Third Annual Phillies Minor League Digest

A Fan's View

Steve Potter

Foreword – Jim Salisbury

Steve Potter's love for the Phillies can be traced to an unexpected matchmaker.

Brace yourself, fans.

My friend Steve was introduced to his great sporting love by ... the hated New York Mets.

Steve was in the fifth grade at New Garden Elementary School in the southeastern corner of Pennsylvania when the MiracleMets of 1969 won the World Series in just their eighth season of existence.

"I didn't know much about baseball back then," Steve recalled. "But our gym teacher, Mr. Brayboy, loved baseball. I remember we watched the World Series in gym class. I remember watching the Mets win the World Series."

Steve was hooked.

Not with the Mets.

With the wonderful game of baseball.

Young Steve soon turned his eye to the local team, the Phillies, and developed a deep affection for that club and a pair of young middle infielders named Larry Bowa and Denny Doyle.

Steve's love for the Phillies and the game continued to grow throughout his youth.

He joined the Kennett Square Little League and made his first trip to Veterans Stadium with young teammates in 1973. His days were filled with baseball, playing for the Kennett High School team and listening to the Phillies on the radio or watching them on TV. He was a student at West Chester University, living at home, when the Phillies won their first World Series in 1980.

"When Tug McGraw struck out Willie Wilson, I woke up the whole house, screaming and carrying on," Steve said. "I went outside and banged pots and pans."

"That is still my favorite memory."

As an adult, Steve, a pitcher/first baseman, attended Phillies Phantasy Camp five times. He was joined by his sons, Dan and Nolan, and son-in-law, Matt, at two camps. He always made sure to wear No. 15 because that was the number worn by his favorite player, Dick Allen. Ask Steve and he'll tell you he felt like a kid the day he got to meet Dick at one camp.

After 32 years in the pharmaceutical industry, Steve retired in 2014, and he and his wife, Barb, moved to Clearwater, the gulf side Florida town that is synonymous with the Phillies. In Clearwater, Steve has continued to passionately follow his favorite team, but his focus has grown beyond the big club. He is a dedicated follower and chronicler of the team's minor-league system and the remarkable book that you are holding in your hands is testament to that.

Steve Potter's third annual Phillies Minor League Digest – A Fan's View – takes you inside the minor-league season and charts the fortunes of all of the franchise's affiliates. It also delves into the passion and drive that fuels every young player's dream to make the majors. Steve doesn't just gather information from box scores and put it into book form. He attends games, extended spring-training games at Carpenter Complex, Gulf Coast League games under the blazing noontime Florida sun, and games in Lehigh Valley, Reading and Lakewood when he comes north for the summer months. When he's not at the games, he's following them on one of his five iPads.

The man is … um … dedicated.

"I watch about 400 games a year," Steve said with a laugh. "It cramps my style when I go in person because I can't watch the other ones."

Steve is a soft-spoken, kind man. I would add that my friend is also incredibly courageous; he has fought the battle of cancer and survived. He is well known around Carpenter Complex, always wearing a red Phillies cap and a smile, always willing to talk about his favorite team and the latest hot shot prospect who "threw the heck out of the ball," on a back field the day before.

Steve's ability to make friends through baseball is extraordinary. Team officials and reporters in Philadelphia look forward to his daily email dispatches from Clearwater. They chronicle the exploits of young men that Steve has gotten to know as players and people. He corresponds regularly with several dozen players throughout the system and is always there with a word of support as they chase their dream. Steve self-publishes this amazing book and prides himself on giving copies to the players he writes about.

"It's my way of giving back," he said. "The majority of these kids won't get to the major leagues so this turns out to be a nice memento for them."

It's a remarkable work, one rooted in love of the Phillies and baseball. I look forward to it arriving each winter. And if you enjoy it as much as I do, you can thank the New York Mets for their role in making Steve Potter a baseball fan.

Jim Salisbury
October 2018

Preface:

This is the third annual Phillies Minor League Digest – A Fan's View. It's a group effort as I've enlisted the help of friends who are as enthusiastic about the Phillies system as I am. Here's a list of the folks who have contributed in producing this year's digest along with the roles they've performed.

Jim Salisbury – NBC Sports Philadelphia Phillies Insider. All Phillies fans know who Jim is, he's an excellent writer and also is featured on NBC Sports Philadelphia broadcasts with his insights and information. It was an honor to have him write this year's foreword for the book.

Jim Peyton – Editor of this book in addition to the primary writer of the reviews in the Gulf Coast League chapter. Jim is the lead writer for Phuturephillies.com. Jim's site covers the Phillies minor leagues each day, it is the foremost fan interactive site in that regard.

Tom Housenick – writer of the team review for the Lehigh Valley IronPigs. Tom is a columnist for The Morning Call in Allentown, PA. He covers the Iron Pigs along with the Phillies major league team as well as high school wrestling. Tom is the guy to follow for Triple A news, follow him at mcall.com/sports and on Twitter @TomHousenick

Jay Floyd – the interview chapter in the book was taken from his website PhoulBallz.com. Jay covers the Phillies minor leagues on his website, the site is an excellent source for player interviews and other Phillies news. Jay can also be found on twitter at @PhoulBallz

Kirsten Karbach – writer of the team review for the Clearwater Threshers. Kirsten is the radio voice of the Threshers and primary writer on Threshersbaseball.com

Steve Dull – writer of the fan's perspective in the Threshers chapter. Steve writes on line about the Phillies Minor Leagues on the site baseballross.wordpress.com. His pen name is Baseball Ross.

The following contributed with photography:

Cheryl Pursell – Cheryl contributes her photos during the season to both the Lehigh Valley IronPigs and the Reading Fightin's. You can follow her on Twitter at @CherylPursell

Michael Dill – the official team photographer for the Lakewood BlueClaws. His website for photography services is michaeldillphotography.com

Mark Wylie – he contributes photos to many of the players upon request, in particular the Gulf Coast League

Gail Dull – photos and her writing can be found on baseballbetsy.wordpress.com. She's "Baseball Betsy"

Danie and Frank Berlingis – they are season ticket holders for the Threshers and have contributed their photos to the cause

Tammi Reibsome – an avid fan of the Williamsport Crosscutters, she's contributed some of her Williamsport photos to the Digest

Barb Potter – my lovely wife, she goes with me to all the games and practices and takes great pictures! She's my biggest supporter.

I write a daily blog on Facebook that covers all aspects of the Phillies with a large focus on the minor leagues. The site is called "The Phillies – A Fan's View". There is also a website link to read the site, you don't have to be a Facebook member to use the link, it is philliesbaseballfan.com. Please give me a follow during the season, it's a labor of love.

We hope you enjoy our collective work, it's all done voluntarily and all store proceeds are contributed to Phillies Charities.

Table of Contents:

Chapter One: Spring Training

Even though Spring Training wasn't slated to start till mid-February many guys came to Carpenter Complex in January to begin workouts. The Phillies partner with the city of Clearwater in a program where minor league players work part time for the Parks and Recreation department in the afternoons. This allows the fellas to work out at the Complex in the mornings. The city works with the Phillies to allow for their baseball routine. This offer is open to all of the minor leaguers albeit there are a limited number of spots.

Pitcher Kyle Young has participated in the program the past couple seasons, he was the first player I saw in January at the Complex. This year pitcher Ben Brown, outfielder Carlos De La Cruz and pitcher Zach Warren also participated.

About mid-January there was a range of 30 to 40 guys working out daily. Dylan Cozens and Roman Quinn were the first of the 40-man roster to arrive. They were both here in early January. My wife Barb and I and our buddy Jim Peyton were there each morning to see the guys go thru their outdoor workouts (usually 9:00 to 11:00) before they dispersed inside for weight training and conditioning. Since the workouts were informal the guys don't wear jerseys with their names on them. Initially, we have to guess the identities of the newest participants until we get to know them.

The new skipper, Gabe Kapler, also was an early arrival. He came to Clearwater in late January. I remember the immediate impact he had on one player in particular. Roman Quinn was unsure of what role he would have with the new regime. The usually affable Quinn was noticeably apprehensive during the early workouts. Kapler pulled

Roman aside behind the cages on Roberts Field the first day he was there. The conversation seemed to lift Roman's spirits and he became his old self again. Later in camp, we saw Quinn get time at shortstop as well as in the outfield. He got a legitimate shot to make the big-league club. That's all he wanted. It's the first time I saw what Kapler would be about. The communication effort on his part was immediately evident and a noticeable strength.

When camp officially opened in mid-February Kapler again demonstrated his openness. He made a point of coming back to Carpenter Complex after addressing the media and chatted with us fans, took pictures, signed autographs and hung out. I've never seen a big-league skipper do that in Spring Training. Early in camp, the minor leaguers train in the afternoons after the big leaguers are done. There aren't many folks who stick around to watch the minor leaguers. We do. I've never seen a big-league skipper come back to the early workouts and watch guys. Kapler did that on multiple occasions. He was all in from the get go. His investment in the job was exemplary from the start. That's the part folks don't often see. We saw it firsthand and in person.

It was my honor this spring training to work with retired Phillies legendary Public Relations Director Larry Shenk. Beginning with the early workouts I would submit a daily story to him which he edited and posted on his blog site philliesinsider.com. We posted stories from early January until camp broke in late March. One of the highlights was the unveiling of Phillies' monuments at their old training site on March 20th at Jack Russell Stadium. The field has been refurbished with updated bleachers, bathrooms and locker facilities. Local college teams now play there along with various high schools. It's also the host site for many tournaments. There was a grand re-opening ceremony with keynote speaker David Montgomery which was emceed by Chris Wheeler. We were on hand for the unveiling of multiple monuments and the opening of the new walkway entitled Monument Park.

The various monuments are in honor of Jack Russell, Robin Roberts, Richie Ashburn, Jim Bunning, Steve Carlton and Mike Schmidt. They have been erected with the reverse side of each marker displaying various tributes to the 1980 World Championship team, other hall of famers who played at the site, as well as the history of the facility.

Jack Russell Memorial Stadium opened in 1955, it was the spring training home to the Phillies until 2004, when they moved to Spectrum Field (formerly Bright House Field). For the event the scoreboard displayed the exact depiction of the score and count for the final pitch of the 1980 World Series. That was really cool. Dickie Noles, a key member of the 1980 team, was on hand to unveil the monument that is in tribute to the 1980 squad.

It was really cool to hear and be on hand for the event. I'm glad the Park continues to host baseball. I've even played there myself in tournament action. If you come to Spring Training it's definitely a place to visit. Especially now with the Phillies version of "Monument Row" now on display!

The Phillies introduced many new approaches this spring. They even held an all hands meeting at the Complex on

January 26th. We got to chat with many of the coaches and front office folks as they walked down from the stadium to the Complex for meetings that day. We patiently sat in the stands and said hello as they passed by. The team owner, John Middleton, stopped and chatted with Jim Peyton and I. It was very evident that he has a great passion and desire to succeed. It was cool he stopped and conversed with two fans, very down to earth.

During Skipper Kapler's first camp we saw a change in practice times to late morning instead of the previous regime's early morning starts. Practices were also shorter in length and had some twists. There were umpires in full attire for bullpen sessions calling balls and strikes. We saw specific drills on pitch framing for the catchers and smaller work groups in general so as to keep the drills crisper. Minor league coaches were brought in early to work the big-league camp. They were needed to conduct the various work stations and to also indoctrinate themselves and align with the new big-league staff. It was different. Some folks didn't like it so much. That would turn out to be a trend as the season progressed it seemed. From my perspective it was refreshing. The old routines had become mundane and this approach at the least was intriguing.

One workout that stood out in particular was an early bullpen that Vince Velasquez threw. It was an electric session as Velasquez was amped and throwing hard. He popped the mitt of catcher Andrew Knapp consistently on the black of the plate that day. The skipper knelt next to Knapp in the batter's box and would key him on how to move his mitt to frame the pitches better. The session was held on the side mounds between Schmidt and Ashburn Fields, so we got to see it up close. It was the first opportunity to witness the process of incorporating what analytics reflected to actual play. The data analysis shows that glove position of the catcher as he receives the ball can positively influence the umpire's call. The working session was translating that data to how Andrew Knapp caught the upper nineties heaters from Velasquez. It's just one of the things they worked on continually during the camp and I'm sure throughout the whole season as well.

Pitchers and catchers reported officially on February 14th and the first game against the University of Tampa was held on the 22nd. It was a 9-0 victory for the Phillies. The official Grapefruit League games started the next day. Daily play went thru March 27th when the final game was played against the Pirates. The spring big league team record for 2018 was 13-17-2. There was a buzz this year, new excitement. The signing of Jake Arrieta during spring certainly contributed to that, along with the great camp that Scott Kingery had and his subsequent signing to a long-term deal. He forced his way onto the opening day roster with his play during spring training. It was evident that the talent on the club was much better than the previous season as camp broke.

Minor league spring training is always held exclusively at the Complex. There are games played there each day as camp progresses. We attended those events when the big club was on the road. Each morning, regardless of where games were played, we watched the minor league workouts. At the end of each camp, three minor league awards are presented. The presentation occurs during the last big-league home game of the spring. This year's award winners were:

Bill Giles Award: Adam Haseley - best American born player in camp

Larry Rojas Award: Simon Muzziotti - best foreign-born player in camp

John Vukovich Award: Rafael DeLima - coaches award for the coach who best exemplified the spirit of Coach Vukovich

This Spring Training camp was the fourth consecutive one we have attended on a daily basis. The first one, back in 2015, was under the direction of Ryne Sandberg and the message then was to be more aggressive, especially as hitters early in the count, for that veteran laden team. In 2016 and 2017 skipper Pete Mackanin oversaw the changeover to more youthful rosters. And here in 2018, under Gabe Kapler, it was "Be Bold" as a challenge to be the "best version of you".

One constant thru all four camps had been the buildup of minor league enthusiasm and talent. Yes, analytics is a dominant feature nowadays and the Phillies have bought in hook, line, and sinker. But, success isn't accomplished by just data analysis. It's also the incorporation into a work environment that breeds a positive outcome, namely, wins.

What I continued to notice in the minor league camp was a workmanlike approach that's been there the past four seasons and a continued evolution of camaraderie. The development staff has been consistent both in approach and personnel. In my humble opinion that familiarity has gone a long way in developing respect and fellowship between the players and the administration.

The players themselves seemingly get along very well with one another. I've seen countless times where guys chide each other in jest but also pick one another up with a fist bump or arm around the shoulders. You can tell friendship by actions, a quick hip check from one pitcher to another when waiting in line for drills, a mock knockout punch to the runner on infield drills followed by big grins, and even more so when a group of guys come sit in the stadium after their work is done to watch their organization mates compete against an opponent.

It's these things I've noticed that continued to make me believe the club is headed in the right direction. Of course, baseball acumen and talent are major elements of the equation but this observer sees that there as well.

Before I retired, I was an executive in Corporate America and led or was part of many major projects. Every one that succeeded had a core engine of inclusion and a consistency of direction with leadership that had clear vision. That's what I've seen developing the past four springs at the levels that most don't observe. The minor leagues are indeed the base of a successful big-league team. My observations of that continually developing base makes me optimistic that a winning success at the big-league level is not only very close but also sustainable.

It's been my pleasure to watch the buildup. Part of me yearns to be a bigger piece of it. I tell myself that I am by writing about what I see each and every day and also by encouraging the young players to persevere and excel. It's why I go to the fields each day I'm able. It's not just the numbers, it's the full experience that builds championships. Watching that makes me appreciate it more. I feel privileged to watch it build. As the young guys say "It's All Part of It". From this observer's views it was a successful spring.

Phun Phact:

If you visited Carpenter Complex this spring you were very likely to meet Don Strohler. He's the security employee of the Phillies who was positioned at the front door of the Paul Owens building. Don was also the gracious greeter of fans, players, executives and anyone else who needs direction. He's a great guy and was always pleasant to talk to.

Don's from Allentown, PA and worked for the Phillies for 15 years. He moved to Florida 25 years ago after retiring from the Allentown Water Department where he was an Operations Supervisor. He's a dad and a granddad with six children (three boys and three girls) and 21 grand kids. His prior residence in Allentown was five minutes from the present site of Coca Cola Park where the IronPigs play.

Don decided to retire after the 2018 season. He reached his 90th birthday and said he wants to just be a fan going forward. We will certainly miss him at the door, but look forward to seeing him at the games. He's a very good man.

Jim Peyton, Don Strohler and myself – Photo by Barb Potter

Chapter Two – Lehigh Valley IronPigs – Tom Housenick

Joey Meneses flirted with the International League's first Triple Crown in 45 years, and then was one of three IronPigs to take home 2018 postseason awards.

Lehigh Valley made the playoff for a third consecutive season by capturing the first North Division title in the franchise's 11-year history. However, the year ended the way the previous two did --- with semifinal losses to rival Scranton/Wilkes-Barre.

On a roster void of any high-ranking major-league prospects, Meneses was among several IronPigs developed into stars who dominated at their respective positions. Meneses, in his only season in the Phillies organization (he was released in late October to pursue an opportunity to play in Japan), led the IL in home runs, RBIs, slugging percentage, OPS, total bases and runs. For his performance, he was voted the IL's MVP and rookie of the year. IronPigs hitting coach Sal Rende, who was among several minor-league hitting instructors let go by the Phillies after the season, and first-year bench coach Wes Helms raved about Meneses' work ethic despite never getting a call-up to the Phillies. Meneses, who spent his first seven professional seasons in the Braves system, never hit lower than .292 in any full month in 2018 and slashed a stellar .347/.394/.554 with two outs and runners in scoring position.

"It's been pretty good, " Rende said of the first baseman/outfielder's impressive two-strike approach. "He can hit the 98-mph fastball. He's on breaking balls. He might swing at a bad breaking ball, but the next one he's going to hit."

Cole Irvin showed a strong mental approach like Meneses. Despite dominating the league, the left-handed pitcher never packed up his locker at Coca-Cola Park for a promotion to the majors. All Irvin did was set a franchise record with an IL-best 14 victories. The 24-year-old also led the league in ERA (2.57), WHIP (1.06) and innings (161 1/3), plus was third in strikeouts with 131. He also posted a string of 13 consecutive starts with at least six innings pitched and allowed one or zero earned runs in seven of his last nine starts. And, instead of being frustrated after seeing teammates Enyel De Los Santos and Ranger Suarez get multiple big-league promotions, Irvin, the IL's pitcher of the year, looked within himself for answers.

"There's something in my development that needs to be done for me to get that call," he said. "It's on me for not getting to that point yet. I just strive to get better every day until that day comes." Irvin's next opportunity for that day should come in spring training with a major-league camp invite.

De Los Santos, the return from the Padres in the Freddy
Galvis trade last winter, proved to be a live arm with
potential as a starter and reliever. In his first Triple-A season,
the 22-year-old Dominican Republic native was 10-5 with a
2.63 ERA and 1.16 WHIP in 22 starts for Lehigh Valley. He had
a 4.74 ERA in seven games (two starts) spanning three
stints with Philadelphia.

De Los Santos topped off at 96-97 mph late in the season for
the IronPigs and Phillies, but it's his short-armed delivery that
deceived hitters.   The right-hander made his MLB debut July
10 in New York against the Mets after earning the starting
pitcher's spot for the International League in the Triple-A All-
Star game and a berth on the International team for the
annual Futures Game later that same week.Four of his five
relief appearances for the Phillies were scoreless outings.

Mitch Walding's seventh professional season was his best.
The third baseman received four call-ups to the majors,
including his MLB debut May 30 in his home state against the
hated Dodgers before playing twice in the stadium (San
Francisco's AT&T Park) he grew up going to. With Lehigh
Valley, Walding put together a solid season, finishing first
in the IL in walks (73), second in OPS (.864), third in OBP
(.390), fifth in slugging percentage (.474) and sixth in home
runs (19) --- all while playing a solid defensive third base.

Dylan Cozens also received multiple call-ups to the Phillies, including his MLB debut on June 1 at San Francisco. He hit his first major-league homer five days later at Chicago's Wrigley Field. The 24-year-old outfielder managed to hit 21 home runs in only 88 Triple-A games with Lehigh Valley. The slugger also posted an .873 OPS in 297 at-bats.

Many of the other significant contributions in 2018 came from a cast of veterans who tasted the major leagues in previous years with other organizations. They were instrumental in the IronPigs' clubhouse chemistry rather than spreading their bitterness at their lack of time in Phillies red pinstripes.

Pedro Beato, Dean Anna, Matt McBride, Collin Cowgill, Trevor Plouffe and Danny Ortiz combined for seven games this year with Philadelphia (all by Plouffe), yet never created a distraction. The cohesiveness may never have been more evident than when Anna hit his only home run of the season in an Aug. 13 home win over Durham. The middle infielder acknowledged the IronPigs bench as he sprinted around first base. As Anna headed for home plate, the players left the dugout and ran down the tunnel toward the clubhouse. Anna, never missing a stride, ran down the dugout steps and into the tunnel to join the brief celebration. Anna's .367 on-base percentage was third-best among qualifying IL batters.

Beato was stellar for a second year in a row as Lehigh Valley's closer, breaking his club record with 35 saves to go with eight wins in an IL-best 63 appearances.

Speedy outfielder Roman Quinn was good enough in a combined 25 games surrounding another injury to earn a trip to the big leagues to stay on July 27.

There were difficult moments in an otherwise smooth ride to the playoffs. Outfielder Andrew Pullin retired in late May after hitting only .171 in 36 games. Left-handed pitcher Brandon Leibrandt was brilliant as a spot starter and reliever for pitching coach Dave Lundquist, setting a franchise record for consecutive scoreless innings (29 2/3) in a year, before being shut down in early July with a season-ending elbow injury that jeopardizes his 2019 season.

And, right-hander Tom Eshelman, the 2017 Paul Owens Award winner as the Phillies organization's top minor-league pitcher, suffered through a miserable 2018: 2-13 record, 5.84 ERA, 1.67 WHIP in 27 games (26 starts). Opponents slashed .321/.368/.502 against the 24-year-old, was remained diligent throughout the most difficult baseball year of his life. Most importantly, he remained a class act and a good teammate.

First-year manager Gary Jones guided the IronPigs through the entertaining 2018 season with a calmness that filtered down to his players. That contributed to the club's 16 comeback wins in the seventh inning or later plus 12 walk-off wins --- including four in a six-day stretch from July 3-8. Jones earned the IL manager of the year award after guiding the IronPigs to an 84-56 record --- the best winning percentage in franchise history. They were in first place every day from June 4 on, had the IL's best record from July 7 on and finished with Triple-A's best record.

What helped this group of IronPigs to such levels of success was Jones' approach, recognizing that winning isn't the only thing. "As you get older, you learn how to better understand that there's more important things in life than winning a baseball game," Jones said. "It's nice to go out and compete. You want to win, but at the end of the day it's not the end of the world if you lose the game."

Here's a look in regards to the IronPigs final team statistical rankings within the 14-team league:

Runs: 3rd - 620
Hits: Tied for 12th - 1,119
Doubles: 10th - 230
Triples: 11th - 21
Home Runs: 1st - 145
RBIs: 3rd - 590
Total Bases: 5th - 1,826
Walks: 1st - 489
Least Strikeouts: 12th - 1,213
Stolen Bases: Tied for 12th - 60
OBP: 4th - .323
Slugging Percentage: 5th - .400
Batting Average: 13th - .245
OPS: 5th - .723

Pitching:

ERA: 4th - 3.63
Shutouts: 3rd - 13
Saves: 2nd - 46
innings Pitched: Tied for 1st - 1,221
Least Hits Allowed: 5th - 1,112
Least Runs Allowed: 5th - 555
Least Earned Runs Allowed: 5th - 492
Least Home Runs Allowed: 9th - 114
Least Walks: 7th - 422
Most Strikeouts: 13th - 1,072
WHIP: Tied for 2nd - 1.26
Holds: Tied for 1st - 59

Individual League Leaders: (in Top 10)

Games: Joey Meneses - Tied for 2nd - 130, Dean Anna - Tied for 7th - 122, Mitch Walding - Tied for 10th - 119

At Bats: Joey Meneses - 4th - 492

Runs: Joey Meneses - Tied for 1st - 75, Dean Anna - Tied for 3rd - 73, Mitch Walding - 5th - 70

Hits: Joey Meneses - 1st - 153

Doubles: Joey Meneses - Tied for 7th - 27

Triples: Dean Anna - 4th - 4

Home Runs: Joey Meneses - Tied for 1st - 23, Dylan Cozens - Tied for 3rd - 21, Mitch Walding - 4th - 19, Danny Ortiz - Tied for 8th - 15

RBIs: Joey Meneses - 1st - 82, Mitch Walding - 8th - 69

Total Bases: Joey Meneses - 1st - 251, Mitch Walding - 10th - 184

Walks: Mitch Walding - 1st - 73, Dean Anna - 8th - 51

Stolen Bases: Roman Quinn - Tied for 9th - 13

OBP (min 2.7 PA/League Game): Mitch Walding - 3rd - .390, Dean Anna - 4th - .367, Joey Meneses - Tied for 7th - .360

Slugging Pct. (min 2.7 PA/League Game): Joey Meneses - 1st - .510, Mitch Walding - 5th - .474

Batting Average (min 2.7 PA/League Game): Joey Meneses - Tied for 2nd - .311

OPS (min 2.7 PA/League Game): Joey Meneses - 1st - .870, Mitch Walding - 2nd - .864

Pitching:

Wins: Cole Irvin - 1st - 14, Enyel De Los Santos - Tied for 4th - 10, Drew Anderson & Tom Windle - Tied for 5th - 9, Pedro Beato - Tied for 6th - 8

ERA (Min .8 IP/League Game): Cole Irvin - 1st - 2.57, Enyel De Los Santos - 2nd - 2.63

Appearances: Pedro Beato - 1st - 63, Tom Windle - Tied for 3rd - 50

Starts: Tom Eshelman - Tied for 2nd - 26, Cole Irvin - Tied for 3rd - 25, Drew Anderson - Tied for 9th - 19

Saves: Pedro Beato - 1st - 35

Innings Pitched: Cole Irvin - 2nd - 161.1, Tom Eshelman - 5th - 140.1, Enyel De Los Santos - 10th - 126.2

Strikeouts: Cole Irvin - 3rd - 131

WHIP (Min .8 IP/League Game): Cole Irvin - 1st - 1.05, Enyel De Los Santos - 2nd - 1.16

Ranger Suarez – Photo by Cheryl Pursell

Pedro Beato – Photo by Cheryl Pursell

Joey Meneses – Photo by Cheryl Pursell

Enyel De Los Santos – Photo by Cheryl Pursell

Tyler Gilbert — Photo by Cheryl Pursell

Cole Irvin – Photo by Cheryl Pursell

Mitch Walding – Photo by Cheryl Pursell

Dylan Cozens – Photo by Cheryl Pursell

Brandon Leibrandt – Photo by Cheryl Pursell

Dean Anna – Photo by Cheryl Pursell

Manager Gary Jones – Photo by Cheryl Pursell

Chapter Three – Reading Fightin's

The 2018 season was a down year in Baseball Town in regards to wins and losses but certainly not in development or fan enthusiasm, Reading was third in total attendance this season marking the 14th consecutive year the Baseball Town faithful have been in the Eastern League's top three for gate support.

The club finished the year with a 64-73 mark (.467) and in fourth place in the six-team eastern division. They were 34-34 on the road and 30-39 at home. Reading was 41-47 before the All-Star break and finished the year with a 23-26 mark. The club went 15-12 during the month of August and 28-25 for July and August combined.

Manager Greg Legg employed 22 different position players and 36 different pitchers during the course of the year. Those numbers included six pitchers and one position player on rehab assignments from the Phillies. Two players (Cord Sandberg and Zach Coppola) retired from baseball during the season, three were released, and five were traded to other organizations. There were twelve players promoted to Lehigh Valley at different points during the year and twelve promoted to Reading from lower levels. The coaching staff had adjustments as well as Greg Brodzinski was added to replace Rico Brogna.

Here's a look at how Reading compared to the other teams in the twelve-team league:

Offense:

Runs: 8th - 600
Hits: 10th - 1,104
Doubles: 12th - 188
Triples: 12th - 17
Home Runs: 1st - 141
RBIs: 8th - 562
Total Bases: 7th - 1,749
Walks: 9th - 417
Least Strikeouts: tied for 9th - 1,158
Stolen Bases - 12th - 62
OBP: 10th - .317
Slugging Pct.: 3rd - .391
Batting Average: 9th - .247
OPS: 9th - .708

Pitching:

ERA: 6th - 4.00
Shutouts: tied for 12th - 5
Saves: tied for 6th - 34
Innings Pitched: 10th - 1,189.2
Least Hits Allowed: 3rd - 1,089
Least Runs Allowed: 6th - 618
Least Earned Runs Allowed: 6th - 529
Least Home Runs Allowed: 7th - 117
Least Hit Batters: 8th - 60
Least Walks Allowed: 12th - 532

Most Strikeouts: 4th - 1,129
WHIP: 5th - 1.36
Holds: Tied for 6th - 34

Individual League Leaders: (in Top 10)

Offense:

Games: Malquin Canelo - tied for 4th - 128

At Bats: Malquin Canelo - 8th - 470

Doubles: Zach Green - tied for 10th - 23

Triples: Malquin Canelo - tied for 2nd - 6

Home Runs: Deivi Grullon - tied for 4th - 21, Zach Green - tied for 6th - 17, Darick Hall & Damek Tomscha - tied for 8th - 15, Jan Hernandez - tied for 9th - 14

Walks - Cornelius Randolph - tied for 10th - 48

Stolen Bases: Malquin Canelo - tied for 4th - 24

OBP (min 2.7 PA/League game): Damek Tomscha - 10th - .352

Slugging Percentage (min 2.7 PA/League game): Damek Tomscha - 8th - .465

Batting Average (min 2.7 PA/League game): Damek Tomscha - 8th - .294

OPS (min 2.7 PA/League game): Damek Tomscha - 8th - .817

Pitching:

Appearances: Edgar Garcia - 4th - 47, Seth McGarry - 7th - 45, Luke Leftwich - tied for 8th - 44

Starts: Harold Arauz - 4th - 24

Saves: Jeff Singer - 4th - 12, Edgar Garcia - tied for 7th - 8

Strikeouts: Harold Arauz - 8th - 113

Standout performers this season:

Malquin Canelo had an "under the radar" season, yet led the Fightin's in six offensive categories (Games, AB's, H, R, TB and stolen bases). He's still a bit erratic with the glove (20 errors) and needs more consistency as a hitter, but the 24-year-old has shown enough to move to triple A next season in my humble view.

Zach Green was able to play a complete season this year and posted good results. The 24-year-old hit .296/.375/.578 with an OPS of .953 at Reading in 77 games with 17 home runs and 53 RBIs. He was promoted to Lehigh Valley on July 12th where he played another 37 games. This was the first time in Zach's seven-year career that he's been able to play over 100 games in a season. Defensively, he split time between first and third base.

Damek Tomscha put up another year of good offensive numbers, .294/.352/.465 with an OPS of .817 in 344 at bats with 15 homers and 54 RBIs at Reading. He also played in 26 games with Lehigh Valley. This was his fifth year in the organization, a solid player.

Catcher Deivi Grullon had an excellent season, he was named a league post season All -Star for hitting .273/.310/.515 with an OPS of .825 in 90 games with 21 home runs and 59 RBIs. Grullon is listed as being 22 years old and has completed his 6th season. Good defensive catchers with some pop are coveted.

Cornelius Randolph blossomed in the second half of the season. He had a stellar July when he posted a slash line of .352/.441/.489 in 26 games and followed that up with a .291/.356/.405 August in 21 games with 4 homers and 24 RBIs. "C" struggled in the first three months of the season but the last two follow the path he's taken as an underage performer thus far in his career at each level. He just turned 21 on June 2nd.

Jan Hernandez started the season like gangbusters with a .327 batting average in April followed by a .307 May. He tailed off the remainder of the season as his playing time diminished. This is Jan's sixth year in the system, it was his best thus far.

Darick Hall led the minor league organization this season in home runs and RBIs. He hit 26 homers and drove in 87 between Clearwater and Reading with 15 home runs and 52 RBIs being at Reading. Darick was chosen to participate in the Arizona Fall League. One of my favorites in the system.

Austin Listi led the minor league organization in both OBP and OPS and was second in batting average. The 24-year-old can flat out hit. He posted a .281/.372/.447 slash line with an OPS of .819 at Reading in 65 games and a line of .312/.412/.502 with an OPS of .915 for the season between Reading and Clearwater with an equally distributed total of 18 home runs. Austin drove in 84 runs this summer, 39 at Reading. Austin also participated in the AFL in the fall.

Adam Haseley has flown up the system ladder. In just his first year of full season play, the 22-year-old had a very strong season. He was promoted from Clearwater to Reading on July 10th and proceeded to tear up the Eastern League with a slash line of .316/.403/.478 in 39 games with 6 homers and 17 RBIs. His full season stats of .305/.361/.433 in 118 games (466 at bats) with 11 home runs and 55 RBIs made for quite an impressive year. He led the entire minor league system in at bats, runs and hits and earned a well-deserved rest for the offseason. Good looking player.

Jose Pujols also had a very strong season. The 22-year-old hit .295/.365/.503 with an .803 OPS in 441 combined at bats between Clearwater and Reading. He stroked 22 home runs and drove in 76 runs. On August 3rd Jose was promoted to Reading and posted solid numbers in the 26 games he played with the Fightin's. He hit .270 with 4 homers and 18 RBIs for Reading. Great bounce back season for Jose!

Pitchers:

Jeff Singer started the season at Clearwater and worked his way back to Reading which is where he left off the year before. He finished the year with Lehigh Valley as part of the playoff roster. Jeff posted 15 saves in 15 chances this summer, 12 at Reading. Big league arm.

Tyler Viza had two excellent months in July and August to close the season. He went 3-1 with a 2.26 ERA in 55 2/3 innings (10 starts) and reestablished himself as a viable candidate for a Lehigh Valley rotation job in 2019. Tyler also pitched in the AFL this fall as part of the Phillies contingent.

Edgar Garcia posted a 7-2 record with an ERA of 3.32 for Reading this season in 59 2/3 IP. It earned the 21-year-old a promotion to Lehigh on August 25th where he became a prominent part of the IronPig bullpen crew for the playoffs. Garcia has an outstanding slider with sharp movement, perhaps the best slider in the system.

Kyle Dohy played at three levels in 2018 beginning at Lakewood and ending at Reading. He posted incredible strikeout numbers with 111 in just 67.1 IP. His ball movement and delivery made him virtually un-hittable as he featured a fastball, slider, and change up. He also walked 42 batters. The 21-year-old has the repertoire to be a big leaguer, just has to harness the command.

JoJo Romero suffered a season ending oblique injury during his best start of the season on July 14th and was placed on the DL on July 20th. The dynamic 21 year old lefty has all the tools to be a very good big league hurler. He possesses a variety of pitches which sort of got in his way this summer as he battled command. Pitching coach Steve Shrenk had him simplify the approach and he started to regain success. JoJo was 7-6 for the season with a 3.80 ERA in 18 starts however he was 2-0 in three starts in July with a stellar 0.90 ERA in 20 IP before the injury.

Josh Tols may possess the biggest downward 12 to 6 breaking curve ball I've seen. The 5'7" Aussie lefty brings the ball seemingly out of his ear in an "iron mike pitching machine" type delivery that's both deceptive and very effective. He will flash the hook anywhere from the high 60's to mid-70's. When coupled with a tailing fast ball sitting at 86-89, he's a real weapon with the uniqueness of his delivery and stuff. He's very effective, his 55 K's in 42.2 IP reflect that.

Connor Seabold was promoted to Reading on June 27th after going 3-0 with a 2.49 ERA for Clearwater during the month. He used a Bronson Arroyo type high leg kick delivery when I saw him in Clearwater but lost command in Reading and coach Shrenk had him simplify it. The 22-year-old righty struggled in June with Reading but bounced back with a 2.79 ERA in five August starts (29 IP).

Luke Leftwich provides a power arm who can furnish length out of the pen, an increasingly more important skill in today's baseball. The 24-year-old has a mid-90's heater with a slider and change up that are effective as well. He continued his development in the fall in the AFL.

Seth McGarry also went to the AFL in the fall and, like Leftwich, is a multi-inning reliever with multiple pitches. He's 24 years old and can heat it up in the mid 90's.

Things picked up a bit in the second half for Reading as an influx of talent came aboard from Clearwater. It was a comparably young crew of players – actually, the youngest average age in the league as a pitching corps at 23.2 and the second youngest set of position players at 23.5. This bodes well for 2019 as some guys may indeed repeat at least the beginning of 2019 with Reading but with the added advantage of the experience gained this season. That's a good thing.

Deivi Grullon – Photo - Michael Dill -Michael Dill Photography

Jan Hernandez – Photo taken by Cheryl Pursell

Adam Haseley – Photo by Cheryl Pursell

Austin Bossart – Photo by Cheryl Pursell

Darick Hall – Photo by Cheryl Pursell

Austin Listi – Photo by Cheryl Pursell

Jeff Singer – Photo by Cheryl Pursell

Josh Tols – Photo - Michael Dill – Michael Dill Photography

Luke Leftwich – Photo by Cheryl Pursell

Zach Green – Photo by Cheryl Pursell

Seth McGarry – Photo by Cheryl Pursell

Edgar Garcia – Photo by Cheryl Pursell

Jose Pujols – Photo by Cheryl Pursell

Damek Tomscha – Photo by Cheryl Pursell

Kyle Dohy – Photo by Cheryl Pursell

Cornelius Randolph – Photo by Cheryl Pursell

Connor Seabold – Photo taken by Cheryl Pursell

Malquin Canelo – Photo taken by Cheryl Pursell

Adam Haseley, Darick Hall, Austin Listi and me – Photo by Barb Potter

Chapter Four – Clearwater Threshers

Kirsten Karbach and Steve Dull

2018 Clearwater Threshers Review By Steve Dull AKA Baseball Ross

The 2018 season was the best season record-wise since we have been Clearwater Threshers' season ticket-holders in 2012. They finished 17 games over .500 and won a playoff game. This was the first playoff win and only the second time in seven years they played in the post season.

It was really a tale of two halves. The Threshers were four games under .500 in the first half and 21 games over .500 in the second half of the Florida State League season. They were first or second in the league for the season in most pitching categories, including first in WHIP. They were third or fourth in most of the offensive categories. With the call-up to Reading of Darick Hall, Austin Listi and Adam Haseley around the half way mark in the season, they fell to sixth in the 12-team league in OPS for the season.

In the first half, the Threshers' power hitters could drive the ball but they did not have as much pitching as they had in the second half. Hall and Listi were FSL All-Stars. Hall hit .277 with a OPS of .904 while leading the league in home runs with 11 after the first 48 games. Listi was second in the FSL in hitting at .347 with 9 homers in 58 games. Haseley hit .300 in 79 games.

The Threshers did lose opening day starter Connor Seabold to a Reading promotion and the highly regarded Sixto Sanchez to an elbow injury to start the second half. However, the overall six-man starting rotation in the second half was outstanding.

The top pitcher in the second half was Mauricio Llovera with his fastball ball sitting at 95-97 mph and a sharp breaking slider at 84 mph. He went 6-1 over the last six weeks of the season and led the Threshers staff in strikeouts for the season. Lefty David Parkinson was called-up from Lakewood and was superb going 3-0 with a 1.29 ERA in five games in August. Ramon Rosso joined the team in the second half and went 6-2. Reliable lefty Bailey Falter went 3-0 with a 0.78 ERA in August. Even highly-regarded Adonis Medina settled down in August, going 1-1 with a 2.57 in the month after putting up a hefty 6.10 ERA in July.

Still, it was the bullpen that preserved the outstanding work of the starting pitching in the second half. The Threshers had the best closer in the league in the second half, Addison Russ. He went 4-0 with a 1.15 ERA and was 14 for 15 in save opportunities. For the season including his work with Lakewood, he was 27 for 28 in save opportunities and went 9-2 with a 1.68 ERA. Jakob Hernandez with 8 holds and Grant Dyer with 5 holds led the way in mostly set-up roles.

We all wondered how the Threshers could score runs in the second half now that Hall, Listi and Haseley were gone. The answers were provided by Grenny Cumana, Luke Williams, Jose Pujols in June and July and Mickey Moniak down the stretch in August and the final two games in September.

Enough cannot be said about the work of Grenny Cumana, who took over in left field in the second half after he did time in extended spring training for the first half. Grenny hit .407 with two homers in June. He also had the most accurate arm in the outfield picking up nine outfield assists in the 46 regular season games he played in the field.

Luke Williams developed into a super sub. In June, he hit .333 with six homers and 20 RBIs. He started at six different positions except pitcher, catcher and shortstop during the season.

In June, right fielder Jose Pujols hit .351 and had an OPS of .979. In July he slugged .600 on his way to hitting seven homers and driving in 21 runs in the month. He was tied with 11 for most outfield assists in the FSL. His play earned him a promotion to Reading for August. Still, he was awarded by the league the 2018 FSL Player of the Year where he slashed at .301/.364/.523 with 18 homers, one triple and 16 doubles in only 95 games.

The Threshers centerfielder Mickey Moniak finished strong in August hitting .311 with a .811 OPS. Look for Mickey to have a big 2019 season.

One of our favorite players was Threshers catcher Henri Lartigue. We always said, "If it was Sunday at 1p.m. in Clearwater, it must be time for Henri Lartigue". He was special when it came to the hot, humid Sunday afternoon games at Spectrum Field. He caught seven Sunday home games during the season and he went 12 for 24, scoring six runs and driving in eight. The Threshers had a 6-1 record in those games, losing only the last Sunday home game in August which Henri was the catcher. It was his only home Sunday game he did not get a hit all season.

One of the highlights of the summer was in back-to-back Sunday games during the end of June and the beginning of July, Henri did something special. He hit a two-run, walk-off homer in the ninth of the first game. Then the next Sunday, he hit a two-run homer in the third inning that held up for a 2-0 win.

While the Threshers won the second half in the Northern Division playing 21 games over .500, the playoffs round were a disappointment. Thanks to Grenny Cumana, the Threshers did win the first game of the best of three semi-final round against Daytona. In the top of the eighth, Cumana threw out the potential lead run at the plate to preserve a 6-6 tie. In the bottom of the eighth, he homered to score the winning run in a 7-6 win at Spectrum Field.

When the series moved to Daytona for the final two games, it looked like the Threshers were all set with ace Mauricio Llovera on the mound. He pitched a one-hitter for six innings protecting a 3-0 lead in the third and deciding game. He yielded a two-run homer in the seventh but Jacob Hernandez came on to end the inning with still a 3-2 Clearwater lead. Trevor Bettencourt, who pitched the eighth inning, surrendered three runs and the Threshers went on to be eliminated by a 5-3 score.

All in all, it was the most interesting season of the seven seasons we have been watching Threshers baseball. Hopefully, someday soon, we will see several of these guys playing at Citizens Bank Park for the Phillies and we will remember when they played so well, for the most part, in the Florida State League.

Season Recap by Kirsten Karbach – Threshers Radio Voice

The final win of 2018 was the most dramatic of the season.

Grenny Cumana spent the first half of the year without a spot on a full-season roster, held back in Extended Spring Training until a chance arose in Clearwater in early June. Cumana had played all of 2017 as an infielder for Clearwater, and had appeared in only 11 games in the outfield in five professional seasons, but embraced the opportunity to serve as a left-fielder for the Threshers during the second half.

Cumana found himself manning left in game one of the FSL North division series on September 4, when the Threshers had seen a 6-2 lead slip through their grasp as Daytona rallied to tie it in the eighth inning. With the go-ahead run at second, Stuart Fairchild singled through the left side, sending Alfredo Rodriguez around third.

Cumana came up firing, and nailed Rodriguez at the plate with a perfect one-hop throw, a do-or-die play that preserved the 6-6 tie.

In the bottom half, Cumana stepped to the plate to lead off. The 5'5" infielder-turned-outfielder - who had just six home runs in his professional career - worked a six-pitch at-bat and hooked a shot down the left field line, clearing the fence for a dramatic, go-ahead home run that proved to be the game-winner in Clearwater's first playoff victory in 11 years.

Although the Threshers came up four wins short of a Florida State League Championship in 2018, Clearwater emerged as the second-half champions in the FSL North and earned its first playoff victory since September 11, 2007.

The 2018 Clearwater Threshers set records for most wins in a month (22-9 in August) and most wins in a half (45-24, second half) dating back to 2004, when the franchise moved to its current location and became known as the Threshers.

The first half was highlighted by one of the top offenses in the Florida State League, featuring the emergence of Phillies 2018 Paul Owens Award winner Austin Listi, the powerful bat of Darick Hall, former first round draft pick Adam Haseley, and 2018 Florida State League Player of the Year Jose Pujols.

A 17th round pick out of Dallas Baptist a year ago, Listi batted .344/.453/.560 with nine homers in an All-Star first half, earning Player of the Week honors on June 17. Listi, 24, was promoted to Double-A Reading the following day, and went on to hit .281 with nine homers in the Eastern League.

Hall, a former Dallas Baptist teammate of Listi's, provided plenty of pop for the Threshers before making the move up to Reading on June 1. Following up an MVP season in the South Atlantic League in 2017, Hall blasted a combined 26 home runs this year, including 11 in 48 games for Clearwater.

Haseley was a consistent force in his first full professional season, batting .300 for Clearwater in 79 games before earning the bump up to Reading on July 10. The eighth overall pick in the 2017 draft out of the University of Virginia, Haseley homered twice in his final five games for Clearwater and hit six more with Reading, finishing with a .305 average and 11 homers combined between the two levels.

Pujols was the league's breakout star in 2018.

A year after batting .194 with eight homers in 90 games for Clearwater, the outfielder emerged as the Florida State League Player of the Year in 2018 after finishing tied for third in the league in average (.301) and second in slugging percentage (.523), while blasting 18 homers and driving in 58 runs in 95 games.

Six Threshers were named to the 2018 FSL North All-Star roster, representing Clearwater in the league's midsummer classic on June 16 at George M. Steinbrenner Field in Tampa. Bailey Falter and Jakob Hernandez each tossed a scoreless inning, while Arquimedes Gamboa earned the starting nod at short and Listi knocked in three runs to help lift the North to a 5-0 win. Sixto Sanchez and Hall were also named to the All-Star squad but did not attend, as Sanchez was injured, and Hall promoted to Reading.

Clearwater opened the second half on a tear, winning six straight on the way to a 9-3 start. With a rotation featuring Adonis Medina, Mauricio Llovera, Bailey Falter, David Parkinson, Alejandro Requena, and Ramon Rosso, Threshers pitching dominated the late stages of the season.

Clearwater's ERA in the month of August was a league-best 2.13 - nearly a run lower than any other team in the FSL. After posting a 4.24 ERA in the first half, the Threshers put up a sparkling 2.98 ERA in the second half.

Jonathan Hennigan and Addison Russ provided an exponential boost out of the bullpen. Hennigan did not allow a run in his first 10 appearances after the southpaw debuted on July 20, and finished with a 1.53 ERA in 15 games. Russ locked down 14 saves in 15 tries - good for third-most in the league - while posting a 1.69 ERA in 29 games.

Clearwater accomplished a rare feat on August 6 in game two of a doubleheader at Tampa.

The Threshers were no-hit by the Tampa Tarpons, but won the ballgame, 1-0 in eight innings, becoming the first Florida State League team in nearly 26 years to win a game in which they were held hitless. The last occurrence in the FSL was in fact the Clearwater Phillies on August 23, 1992, as part of a double no-hitter in which the Phillies managed to defeat Scott Bakkum and the Winter Haven Red Sox, 1-0.

Per the new extra-inning rule - as it was a doubleheader, the game was originally slated for seven innings - Luke Williams started the eighth inning at second base. After advancing to third on an error, Williams scored on Daniel Brito's grounder to first for the only run of the night.

Off the field, the Threshers unleashed the new Dog Days of Summer promotion, where fans were encouraged to bring their dogs out to the ballpark during every Sunday home game. Dog tickets were available for six dollars, and proceeds from each dog ticket sold benefitted a local pet charity.

This season also featured the debut of What Could Have Been Night. On August 24, the Threshers became the Clearwater Beach Dogs, with specialty jerseys, hats, merchandise, and food items for one night only, including lobster mac & cheese hotdogs, bacon-wrapped hotdogs with grilled pineapple, and drinks such as margaritas and rum runners with a popsicle.

Spectrum Field welcomed 181,686 fans in 2018, as the Threshers achieved the league's highest attendance for the eighth consecutive year. July 3rd's stunning fireworks display drew the largest crowd of the season, as 9,857 witnessed a 3-2 Threshers win over the Lakeland Flying Tigers.

From a dominant second half to a playoff berth, a comeback story to a heroic performance, and from the Dog Days to the Beach Dogs, 2018 packed in the excitement at Spectrum Field.

Here's a look in regards to the Thresher's final team statistical rankings within the 12-team league:

Offense:

Runs - tied for 5th with Palm Beach at 592 (an average of 4.3 per game)
Hits - 3rd with 1,185 (an average of 8.6 per game)
Doubles - 6th with 200
Triples - 4th with 34
Home Runs - 4th with 87
RBIs - 5th with 541
Total Bases - 4th with 1,714
Walks - tied for 8th with 382 (an average of 2.8 per game)
Least Strikeouts - 5th with 1,021
Stolen Bases - 13th with 66
OBP - 6th at .322
Slugging Pct - 5th at .374
Batting Average - 3rd at .258
OPS - 6th at .696

Pitching:

ERA - 4th at 3.60
Shutouts - 1st with 14
Saves - tied for 2nd with 37
Innings Pitched - 1st with 1,193
Least Hits Allowed - 6th with 1,073
Least Runs Allowed - tied for 5th with 546
Least Home Runs Allowed - 13th with 91
Least Hit Batters - 12th with 78
Least Walks Allowed - 6th with 400
Most Strikeouts - 2nd with 1,212

WHIP - 1st at 1.23
Holds - 2nd with 41

Individual League Leaders: (in Top 10)

Offense:

At Bats - Arquimedes Gamboa - 9th - 434, Mickey Moniak - 10th - 433
Hits - Mickey Moniak - 5th - 117
Doubles - Mickey Moniak - 3rd - 28
Home Runs - Jose Pujols - tied for 3rd - 18, Darick Hall - tied for 7th - 11, Austin Listi & Luke Williams - tied for 9th - 9
RBIs - Jose Pujols - 10th - 58
Total Bases - Jose Pujols - 5th - 184, Mickey Moniak - tied for 10th - 166
Walks - Arquimedes Gamboa - 5th - 53
OBP (minimum 2.7 PA per league game) - Jose Pujols - 6th - .364
Slugging Pct. (minimum 2.7 PA per league game) - Jose Pujols - 2nd - .523
Batting Average (minimum 2.7 PA per league game) - Jose Pujols - 3rd - .301
OPS (minimum 2.7 PA per league game) - Jose Pujols - 2nd - .887

Pitching:

Wins - Adonis Medina - tied for 4th - 10, Bailey Falter & Mauricio Llovera - tied for 6th - 8th
ERA (minimum .8 IP/League Game) - Mauricio Llovera - 7th - 3.72, Adonis Medina - 9th - 4.72
Appearances - Jakob Hernandez - 3rd - 43

Saves - Addison Russ - 3rd - 14
Innings Pitched - Mauricio Llovera - 7th - 121
Strikeouts - Mauricio Llovera - 1st - 137, Adonis Medina - 3rd - 123
WHIP - (minimum .8 IP/League Game) - Mauricio Llovera - 2nd - 1.11, Adonis Medina - 5th - 1.25
Holds - Jakob Hernandez - 3rd - 8, Jonathan Hennigan - 5th - 6, Grant Dyer - 7th - 5
Games Finished - Addison Russ - 4th – 25

Standout performers this season:

Adam Haseley - hit .300/.343/.415 in 79 games (330 at bats) before his promotion to Reading <u>on July 10th</u>

Austin Listi - hit .344/.453/.560 in 58 games (209 at bats) before his promotion to Reading <u>on June 18th</u>

Darick Hall - hit .277/.367/.538 with 11 home runs and 35 RBIs in 48 games (173 at bats) before his promotion to Reading <u>on June 1st</u>

Jose Pujols - hit .301/.364/.523 with 18 home runs and 58 RBIs in 95 games (352 at bats) before his promotion to Reading on August 3rd

Mickey Moniak - hit .311/.355/.456 in the month of August and .295 for July and August combined

David Parkinson - 3-0 with a 1.24 ERA in five games with Clearwater, 11-1 with a 1.45 ERA in 22 games (124.1 IP) combined with Lakewood

Raymond Rosso - 6-2 with a 2.91 ERA in eleven games with Clearwater, 11-3 with a 2.03 ERA in 23 games (123.1 IP) combined with Lakewood

Addison Russ - 4-0 with 14 saves and a 1.69 ERA in 29 games (32 IP) with Clearwater, 9-2 with a 1.68 ERA in 54 games (64.1 IP) with 27 saves combined with Lakewood.

Jonathan Hennigan - 1.53 ERA with 6 holds in 15 games (17.2 IP) with Clearwater, 1-1 with 2.39 ERA (52.2 IP) with 13 holds combined with Lakewood

Jakob Hernandez - 3-3 with a 2.80 ERA in 43 games (70.2 IP) with 92 K's, 8 holds and 5 saves

Trevor Bettencourt - 0.53 ERA in 10 games (17 IP) with 21 K's and 4 holds since coming off the DL on 8/4/18

Bailey Falter - 8-4 with a 2.69 ERA in 17 games (93.2 IP)

Sixto Sanchez - 4-3 with a 2.51 ERA in 8 games (46.2 IP)

Kyle Dohy - 2-1 with a 1.64 ERA in 7 games (11 IP - 18 K's) before being promoted to Reading on July 14th

Adonis Medina went 10-4 in 22 games (111.1 IP) with 123 K's

Mauricio Llovera went 4-0 in August with a 1.74 ERA in 5 games (31 IP) with 38 K's and 5 BB's

Adam Haseley – Photo by Gail Dull – AKA Baseball Betsy

Austin Listi – Photo by Gail Dull – AKA Baseball Betsy

Jakob Hernandez – Photo by Gail Dull – AKA Baseball Betsy

Addison Russ – Photo by Gail Dull – AKA Baseball Betsy

Jonathan Hennigan – Photo by Gail Dull – AKA Baseball Betsy

Kevin Markham – Photo by Danie Berlingis

Bailey Falter – Photo by Gail Dull – AKA Baseball Betsy

Trevor Bettencourt – Photo by Frank Berlingis

Jose Pujols – Photo by Michael Dill – Michael Dill Photography

Adonis Medina – Photo by Gail Dull – AKA Baseball Betsy

David Parkinson – Photo by Gail Dull – AKA Baseball Betsy

Mickey Moniak – Photo by Gail Dull – AKA Baseball Betsy

Ramon Rosso – Photo by Gail Dull – AKA Baseball Betsy

Mickey Moniak with a great catch! – Photo by Mark Wylie

Darick Hall – Photo by Michael Dill – Michael Dill Photography

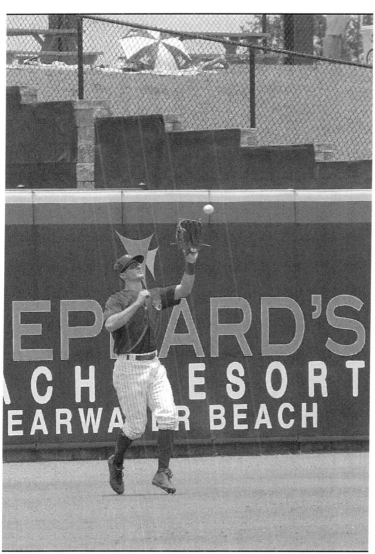

Luke Williams – Photo by Mark Wylie

Sixto Sanchez – Photo by Michael Dill – Michael Dill Photographing

Henri Lartigue – Photo by Gail Dull – AKA Baseball Betsy

Grenny Cumana – Photo by Danie Berlingis

Playoff celebration after clinching second half title

Chapter Five – Lakewood BlueClaws

Lakewood won both season halves of the South Atlantic League Northern Division (41-28 first half, 46-23 second half, 87-51 overall).

The BlueClaws set a franchise record for wins this season and were second in all of minor league baseball in wins and winning percentage trailing only Bowling Green of the Midwest League in both categories.

Manager Marty Malloy used twenty-two different position players this season and twenty-three different pitchers. There were two position players promoted to Clearwater during the summer and three promotions accepted from Williamsport. Amongst the pitchers, five were promoted to Clearwater and two were added near the end of the season from Williamsport. One position player (Colby Fitch) took the hill during regular season play. Only one player off the roster was released from the organization during the summer.

In the playoffs, the BlueClaws swept Kannapolis two games to none in the semifinals to advance to the SAL Championship Series where they lost to Lexington, two games to one. The highlight of the playoffs was a no hitter tossed by Spencer Howard in a 1-0 victory. Howard was spectacular. The right hander struck out nine batters, walked just one and hit a batter.

Howard hit 100 MPH with his fast ball on multiple pitches early in the game. His fastball sat 94-98 with 96 being the most consistent velocity. He threw 103 pitches, 73 for strikes.

Only three BlueClaws have thrown all nine in a no-hitter:

1. Gavin Floyd (2002, a loss)
2. Nick Fanti (2017)
3. Spencer Howard (2018)

Here's a look in regards to the BlueClaws final team statistical rankings within the 14-team league:

Offense:

Runs: 10th - 543
Hits: 8th - 1,105
Doubles: Tied for 6th - 230
Triples: 11th - 28
Home Runs: Tied for 4th - 95
RBIs: 9th - 492
Total Bases: 7th - 1,676
Walks: 10th - 355
Least Strikeouts: 2nd - 1,019
Stolen Bases: 10th - 80
OBP: Tied for 9th - .313
Slugging Pct: 5th - .381
Batting Average: 6th - .251
OPS: 8th - .694

Pitching:

ERA: 1st - 2.74
Complete Games: 1st - 7
Shutouts: 1st - 23
Saves: 1st - 49
Innings Pitched: 4th - 1,172.2
Least Hits Allowed: 1st - 979

Least Runs Allowed: 1st - 433
Least Earned Runs Allowed: 1st - 357
Least Home Runs Allowed: 1st - 63
Least Hit Batters: 2nd - 48
Least Walks: 8th - 380
Most Strikeouts: 1st - 1,305
WHIP: 1st - 1.16
Holds: 3rd - 31

Individual League Leaders: (in Top 10)

Offense:

Hits: Jake Scheiner - 4th - 134
Doubles: Jake Scheiner - 5th - 30, Nick Maton - Tied for 9th - 26
Triples: Jake Scheiner and Nick Maton - Tied for 4th - 5
Home Runs: Rodolfo Duran - Tied for 5th - 18
RBIs: Jake Scheiner - 7th - 67
Total Bases: Jake Scheiner - 4th - 213
Walks: Jake Scheiner - Tied for 6th - 49, Nick Maton - Tied for 10th - 43
OBP (min 2.7 PA/League game): Jake Scheiner - 1st - .372
Slugging Percentage (min 2.7 PA/League game): Jake Scheiner - 7th - .470
Batting (min 2.7 PA/League game): Jake Scheiner - 2nd - .296
OPS (min 2.7 PA/League game): Jake Scheiner - 4th - .842

Pitching:

Wins: Damon Jones - Tied for 2nd - 10, Spencer Howard - Tied for 3rd - 9, David Parkinson & Will Stewart -Tied for 4th - 8 , Julian Garcia - Tied for 5th – 7

ERA (minimum 0.8 IP/League Game): Will Stewart - 2nd - 2.06, Damon Jones - 10th - 3.41

Appearances: Zach Warren - 6th - 39

Starts: Spencer Howard - Tied for 4th - 23, Damon Jones - Tied for 5th - 22, Will Stewart - Tied for 7th – 20

Complete Game Shutouts: Will Stewart - Tied for 1st - 2
Saves: Zach Warren - 2nd - 15, Addison Russ - Tied for 3rd – 13

Strikeouts: Spencer Howard - Tied for 1st - 147, Damon Jones - Tied for 6th – 123

WHIP: (minimum 0.8 IP/League Game) - Will Stewart - 2nd - 0.98

Holds: Connor Brogdon & Julian Garcia - Tied for 5th - 5, Luis Carrasco, Jonathan Hennigan and Zach Warren - Tied for 6th - 4

Standout performers this season:

Jake Scheiner led the team in twelve offensive categories: Games - 122, At Bats - 453, Runs - 65, Hits - 134, Doubles -30, Triples - 5, RBIs - 67, Total Bases - 213, Bases on Balls - 49, OBP - .372, Batting Average - .296, OPS - .842

Matt Vierling was very productive in the 50 games he played for Lakewood: .293/.342/.473 with an .842 OPS, 15 doubles, 6 homers and 25 RBIs after his promotion from Williamsport on July 2nd. Overall, he hit .321/.365/.496/.860 with 18 doubles, 7 homers, and 31 RBIs in 62 games (234 at bats) in his first pro season.

Nick Maton hit .310/.378/.494 during the month of July in 87 at bats. He played a solid shortstop all season in 939 innings at the position and posted a .966 fielding percentage in 437 chances. He hit a solid .256 for the season in 406 at bats with 8 homers and 51 RBIs

Rodolfo Duran had a very solid season as the primary catcher for the club. The 20-year-old hit a team high 18 home runs and also led the club in slugging percentage (.495). Defensively, he posted a .995 fielding percentage and threw out 39 would be base stealers out of 93 attempts (42 %). He also stroked 17 doubles and handled the league's best pitching staff without pause. Great season for the young man.

Kevin Markham hit .310/.365/.379 in the month of June and posted a .282/.353/.376 slash line in 53 games (170 at bats)

with the BlueClaws. In the month of July, he hit .432 for Clearwater after being promoted (16 for 37) and finished the combined year with a solid .269/.339/.351 slash line in 98 games (308 at bats) with 17 stolen bases.

Pitchers:

David Parkinson - 8-1 with a 1.51 ERA in 17 starts (95.1 IP) with Lakewood with 115 Ks, 11-1 with a 1.45 ERA in 22 games (124.1 IP) combined with Clearwater.

Raymond Rosso - 5-1 with a 1.33 ERA in 12 starts (67.2 IP) with Lakewood with 81 K's, 11-3 with a 2.03 ERA in 23 games (123.1 IP) combined with Clearwater.

Addison Russ - 5-2 with 13 saves in 13 chances and a 1.67 ERA (32.1 IP) with 37 K's with Lakewood, 9-2 with a 1.68 ERA in 54 games (64.1 IP) with 27 saves combined with Clearwater.

Jonathan Hennigan - 2.83 ERA in 22 games (35 IP) with 2 saves and 4 holds. He posted a 2.08 ERA in the second half including a 1.13 ERA in the month of July with Lakewood, 1-1 with 2.39 ERA (52.2 IP) with 13 holds combined with Clearwater

Kyle Dohy - posted a 0.80 ERA in 24 games (33.2 IP) with 7 saves and 63 K's with Lakewood. He recorded 111 K's in 67.1 IP combined for the year combined with Clearwater and Reading and posted an overall ERA of 2.54 with 10 saves.

Will Stewart - went 8-1 with a 2.06 ERA in 20 games (113.2 IP) with 90 K's and a WHIP of 0.98 which led all starters in the Organization.

Zach Warren - posted 15 saves after taking over the closer role in the second half. His ERA for the season was 1.91 in 39 games (56.2 IP) with 100 strikeouts. He had an outstanding second half of the season with a 0.68 ERA in 21 games (26.1 IP) with a 2-1 record and 14 saves with 56 K's. He was lights out!

Andrew Brown - went 6-3 with a 2.10 ERA in 14 games (68.2 IP) with 58 K's and a WHIP of 0.95.

Gustavo Armas - 3-1 with a 2.32 ERA in 8 starts (50.1 IP) with 47 K's and just 9 walks after being promoted from Williamsport.

Connor Brogdon - 5-3 with a 2.47 ERA in 31 games (69.1 IP) with 79 K's and just 16 walks. He had 5 saves and 5 holds. He also had a stellar second half when given the opportunity to pitch more, a 0.89 ERA in 20 games (30.1 IP) with 40 K's and just 6 walks. He posted all 5 of his saves in the second half. Connor posted a 0.00 ERA in 8 games in July (12 IP), a 0.69 ERA in August (8 games - 13 IP).

Julian Garcia went 7-3 with a 3.54 ERA in 28 games (8 starts - 78 IP) with 94 strikeouts. He made all 8 starts in the second half and went 5-2 with a 2.17 ERA in 14 games (54 IP) with 66 strikeouts. He was stellar in August with a 1.80 ERA in 5 starts (30 IP - 36 K's).

Damon Jones - went 10-7 with a 3.43 ERA in 23 games (22 starts) with 123 K's in 113.1 IP. He dominated in May with a 1.17 ERA for the month in 23 IP and again in June with a 1.46 ERA in 24.2 IP.

Luis Carrasco had a solid season for the BlueClaws, he went 5-2 with a 3.11 ERA in 66.2 IP and converted 4 of 7 save opportunities. Luis struck out 59 batters and walked 27 in the 30 games in which he appeared. The twenty-four-year-old right hander has upper 90's velocity.

As can be seen, it was a pitching dominated season for the BlueClaws with a lot of contributors. Guys who weren't getting innings in the first half due to outstanding performances by others, made their own outstanding performances in the second half. Great pitching depth on this club and "little league dominant numbers" as Tommy Greene would say. Just an outstanding season for Lakewood, if these guys continue to post numbers like this as they advance, it bodes very well for the Phillies future!

Rodolfo Duran – Photo – Michael Dill - Michael Dill Photography

Zach Warren – Photo – Michael Dill – Michael Dill Photography

Connor Brogdon – Photo – Michael Dill - Michael Dill Photography

Damon Jones – Photo – Michael Dill - Michael Dill Photography

Jake Scheiner – Photo – Michael Dill - Michael Dill Photography

Jhailyn Ortiz – Photo – Michael Dill – Michael Dill Photography

Edwin Rodriguez – Photo – Michael Dill - Michael Dill Photography

Danny Brito – Photo – Michael Dill - Michael Dill Photography

David Parkinson – Photo – Michael Dill - Michael Dill Photography

Nick Maton – Photo – Michael Dill - Michael Dill Photography

Simon Muzziotti – Photo – Michael Dill - Michael Dill Photography

Andrew Brown – Photo – Michael Dill - Michael Dill Photography

Colby Fitch – Photo – Michael Dill - Michael Dill Photography

Julian Garcia – Photo – Michael Dill – Michael Dill Photography

Jonathan Hennigan – Photo – Michael Dill - Michael Dill Photography

Will Stewart – Photo – Michael Dill - Michael Dill Photography

Matt Vierling – Photo – Michael Dill - Michael Dill Photography

Kyle Dohy – Photo – Michael Dill - Michael Dill Photography

Kyle Young – Photo by Jay Floyd – the lefty battled injuries in 2018, looking for a bounce back season in 2019.

Chapter Six – Player Interviews – Jay Floyd

The following excerpts are from the website PhoulBallz.com which is written and operated by Jay Floyd. On the tab "about" tab on the site a background on Jay is written. Here's the content of that tab.

"Jay Floyd's grandfather drove the Phillies' bus for regional road trips during the 1960's. Since those days, baseball was in the family.

In the past decade, Jay has spent time as a coach to teenage players, as a minor league reporter and as a weekly radio analyst during the professional baseball season.

His web site, PhoulBallz.com, served as a launching pad for Jay to start writing about the great sport and the site's affiliation with the Townsquare Media group's Shore Sports Network allowed Jay to cover local minor league clubs, like the Lakewood BlueClaws, from the inside.

Jay is a published writer and photographer in a freelance capacity and he spent more than six years with PhilliesNation.com as a minor league contributor. As PhilliesNation grew and debuted its weekly television program in 2012, Jay was also regularly featured as a correspondent and panelist on the show.

Additionally, Jay co-hosted a successful internet radio show, known as The PhoulBallz Minor League Podcast, along with Tug Haines. That show, which featured live call-in interviews and in-studio guests would garner thousands of weekly downloads during its time in production.

During his time covering baseball, Jay has interviewed various players, coaches and team personnel from the minor leagues to the Majors, including All-Stars, Cy Young Award winners, team executives as well as Hall of Famers."

Here are two interview articles Jay did from this season, one with Jose Pujols and the other with Connor Brogdon. They are also from his web page. I always find his articles to be great reads. I encourage all Phillies minor league fans to read PhoulBallz.com, it's good stuff!

Jose Pujols – Interview article from September 2nd

Following a pair of up and down years, Phillies outfield prospect Jose Pujols has taken strides to improve his approach as well as his outlook and the positive results have been apparent.

Two seasons ago he looked like a promising slugger who made improvements. Last year he moved up a level and appeared to struggle. This year he's returned to resembling a talented player on the rise and he's focus on staying on that path.

Pujols, signed as an international free agent at the age of 16 in 2012, was always promising, but showed he could be a powerhouse during his first year of full-season baseball in 2016. As a member, then, of the Class A Lakewood BlueClaws, the six-foot-three 175-pounder set that club's single-season home run record at the time with a mark of 24. Overall in 128 games in the South Atlantic League that year, Pujols tallied a .241 batting average with 82 runs batted in.

He would move up to Class A Advanced Clearwater last year and his offense looked troubling. He batted .194 with just eight home runs and 29 RBI in 90 games for the Clearwater Threshers.

His manager, Shawn Williams, who had coached Pujols at three different levels, earning promotions along with him from Class A short-season Williamsport, to Lakewood and then to Clearwater, never saw his opinion of Pujols take a slip.

"He always told me, 'You are a leader and don't forget that!'," Pujols shared. "He has always been around me and reminding me of the type of player that I am and the type of player that I can become."

Asked if he feels like a leader around his peers and teammates, the right-handed batter describes leading by example.

"It's like something that you feel. I just want to always see my teammates playing hard. I will always be there for them. Maybe one time you're not hitting well, but there's always something you can do to help your team stay in the game. There's always something you can do. Maybe a good play, or maybe a good cut off and a relay, or a diving catch, or base running. There's always going to be something you can do to help them out," Pujols said.

This year, opening the season repeating the Florida State League, Pujols really turned things around. In 95 games with the Threshers he recorded a .301 average, blasted 18 home runs and drove in 58.

The outstanding production earned him a promotion to Double-A Reading, where he's posted a .274 average with four homers and 18 RBI through 24 contests in the Eastern League.

The improvement this year is something that Pujols credits partly to an adjustment with his hands and where he holds the bat, but he feels that his statistical rebound was more between his ears. He describes having a better plan and a more solid approach at the plate being critical to his development. Understanding more of what the opposing pitcher is trying to accomplish as well supports his goals at the plate.

Striking out a considerable amount has become something that Pujols, like many power hitters, is known for. This is evident with strike out percentages in recent years: 32.6% in 2016 with Lakewood, 42.6% last year in Clearwater and 33.1% at the combined two levels this season. Though, he doesn't focus on this particular result

"I don't think about the strike outs at all. I just think about (sticking) with my plan because when you have a plan, good thing can happen," Pujols stated. "When you have a plan, you've got a better chance to put a ball in play and you know what you're trying to do.'

In his first three years of pro ball as a teenager, Pujols played short-season leagues, combining for a .221 average with 15 home runs and 81 RBI over 168 games, part of that time with Williams, the son of former big-league manager Jimy Williams, in Williamsport.

Pujols looks at Williams as a father figure and credits him for remaining a believer and a supporter in his abilities.

When the pair first met, Pujols didn't know how to play pepper, a common drill or game that helps players develop hand-eye coordination. Williams mentions that instance to Pujols on occasion as a reminder of how far the young man has come in the game.

A father himself, Pujols has a toddler son in the Dominican Republic. For Pujols, the past couple of seasons as a parent have been difficult. He does his best to communicate with his son often and values every moment he can with his child. Pujols looks forward to a lasting career in baseball that will allow him to bring his son to the United States.

It's his love for the game, as well as his son, that drives him. The boy is named after Yankees great Derek Jeter. Jose and his brother Cristopher, a minor leaguer in the Mets organization, admired the future Hall of Famer so much that they had an agreement during childhood that the first of them to have a son would name him after Yankees all-time hits leader.

What stood out to Pujols so much about Jeter was his respect for the game. A respect that Pujols holds with considerable regard on the field every day, even including umpires in his focus and approach to the game.

"Everything between the lines is one thing," Pujols expressed. "Sometimes (I may want to express displeasure to an umpire) when I feel mad about something, but I just let it go, because after all they are people and they can make mistakes and there is no way that people don't make mistakes. You're all going to make mistakes once in a while. So, I just let it go and go back to my game and have fun."

With that kind of consideration and outlook, Pujols seems to have the makings of a very good dad. Furthermore, the more he can influence those around him, prevail on the diamond and pepper the opposition, the more fun and success Pujols is bound to enjoy in the Phillies developmental system.

Jose Pujols – Photo – Michael Dill – Michael Dill Photography

Connor Brogdon – August 24th Interview

Right-handed pitcher Connor Brogdon has been a key part of the Class A Lakewood pitching staff all year long. After opening the 2018 campaign in the starting rotation, and posting a 1-2 record with a 3.73 ERA over seven starts, the 23-year-old was moved into a relief role, where he has been excellent. In 21 relief appearances, Brogdon has tallied a 4-1 record with four saves, a 1.64 ERA, a .190 batting average against and a 12.0 K/9 mark.

A 10th round draft pick last year out of Lewis-Clark State (the same school that produced former Phillies farm hand Tyler Knigge) by the Phillies, Brogdon, a California native, is listed at 6-feet-6-inches tall and 192 pounds.

I spoke with Brogdon recently about his team's excitement level for the upcoming South Atlantic League playoffs, his refined pitch repertoire, the role changes he's undergone this season and plenty more. Read ahead for that full interview.

-I just wanted to get some thoughts on your spot right now...as you've changed roles throughout the season.

So, obviously I was a starter at the beginning of the year. I switched roles and went to the bullpen when Kyle Young came up. And then I was kind of a long relief guy because I was fresh out of starting. And then most of the second half I've been a late inning guy to bridge the gap to get to Zach Warren (the closer) and hold the lead in tight situations. It's been a lot of fun coming into situations like that.

-Is this something you feel has made you more versatile or valuable?

Yeah, definitely. I think I've pretty much proved that I can do both. I can start and come into tight ball games and even get a save here and there when Zach has pitched the previous night. So, yeah, I think I've shown that I can be versatile in the 'pen for sure.

-What's the pitch menu for you? What's the full repertoire and what do you consider your go-to pitch?

I've got a fastball, I've got a slider, change up and then I'm working on a new curve ball. I had one, kind of lost the feel for it, so now I'm working with Zach on his, 'cause his is really good. So, I'm trying to kind of almost mimic it. And it's coming along. But my go-to is my fastball and my change up. And I'll show the slider here and there to mostly righties and very seldomly to lefties.

-With the update to the curve ball, is that a refined grip?

Yeah, I changed my grip. Zach throws a spike curve, so I basically just completely copied his grip and I'm just toying around with it, seeing if it'll play. I've only busted it out twice, two different pitches in a game and they were both in the dirt, so it's got a ways to go.

-The big story with the team this season has been its outstanding pitching that has led the league in staff ERA for a huge majority of the year. What is it like to be a big part of that?

It's a lot of fun. I think we've got a good thing going here. Every single starter on this squad has been extremely solid and you know you can count on getting five to seven strong innings out of them. And then coming out of the bullpen, it's just our job to pick up where they left off and hold the lead for them and keep the offense in the game.

-I've talked to a lot of the pitchers on this team and some guys will talk about the unity and the support that each member of the staff supports and helps one another. Do you find that same thing, where nobody is the selfish type and everyone's looking out for the next guy?

Yeah, definitely. I think we're all looking out for each other and in my personal case when I go to Zach and I ask him, "What can I do to make my curve ball better?" He doesn't hesitate to help and give me queues to help develop the pitch and I think it's like that with a lot of guys. You can ask anybody for anything as far as improving a certain pitch or their approach or their mindset and they'll be willing to help out.

-The feedback I've heard on your pitching coach Brad Bergesen is that sometimes he'll lay off and allow you guys to independently work and sort of coach yourselves. Is that freedom part of what allows you to go work on a new offering or is he hands-on with that?

Yeah, he lets us go on our own, but he's always there. I've gone over film several times with him. He stands in on my flat-grounds when I need him to, 'cause I've been working on throwing the breaking ball at the back foot of a lefty, so he'll stand in left-handed and let me have a visual. He's always there. But there is a certain sense of free reign kinda like "explore yourself", but he's always there when you need him and he's a very knowledgeable guy.

-What's the vibe of late? Is the grind of the long season a big factor right now?

Yeah, you know, it's August. It's been a long stretch. You can tell it's getting toward the end of the year. But, we know that playoffs are coming up and only as of late have we been on a little bit of a skid, with losing four straight to Lexington. But I mean, we've kept it rolling all season till now, so I'm sure we'll turn it around when we go on the road to Hickory and Greensboro.

-It's been a while since the team clinched the playoff spot with the first half title. Is the excitement for the postseason still there?

Yeah, definitely. We keep it pretty fun all the time in the clubhouse and on the field. You know, we're having a lot of fun. Especially when we're winning. Like I said, this is the first series we've been swept- I could be wrong (about that), but we're having a lot of fun. Coming in the clubhouse every day is exciting. A lot of music being played after games most times, 'cause we're winning and only as of late has it been quiet. But I'm sure on the road, we'll turn it around pretty quick.

-When there are these lulls with the long season or following a series sweep, who is the guy on this team that's going to pick everybody up?

I think we've got a few guys. I think Quincy Nieporte, he's a pretty vocal guy. Colby Fitch also pretty vocal. You know, they're always talking. They're always keeping everybody's heads up. Zach Warren out of the bullpen. He's another vocal guy. He's one of those guys that keeps it light. He's really funny. He cracks a lot of jokes. It's hard to be extremely serious and it's a good thing. I mean even (manager) Marty (Malloy) and coach Bergesen, they talk a lot. They're on us. You know, stern when they need to be, but they'll also keep it light.

-What had it been like for you here this season? What do you like about New Jersey?

Definitely different. I kind of like the Wawas. Big Wawa guy. Weather's different. Where I'm from, the west coast, it's pretty dry. Here it's humid. I've seen a lot of rain this year. Don't get to see that a lot where I'm from. It's been fun. I've enjoyed it. Especially the Wawa, the pork roll, egg and cheese. It's all good.

-Now the pork roll, egg and cheese is a big thing here with the mascot races each game. Which one are you partial to, with the races that go on?

I usually root for whoever is last in the standings, 'cause I figure they have the best chance of winning. But, I've been a big cheese guy this year, I think.

-I also wanted to ask you if there were any players or pitchers that you admired while growing up. Was there anyone that you wanted to emulate?

Jose Fernandez. I really tried to model my game after him as I was coming up through junior college and then in college. And he recently passed, but I really tried to model myself after him. He probably wasn't as tall as me, but he still had an electric slider and I tried to adopt that as much as I could. It'll probably never look like that, but that's one guy that I really watching a lot, coming up.

-Did you collect baseball cards growing up?

No, not really.

-Is there any early baseball memory that sticks out for you? Or was there a point when you realized that this could be a possibility to play pro ball?

I just know I came from a small town and I was always one of the better players on the team and I was actually a catcher and third baseman and I wasn't a pitch until later. And I just remember I always hit for power. Hit a lot of home runs. I really enjoyed hitting home runs and being the feared hitter on the team when I was coming up through little league and stuff.

-Do you ever take batting practice out here to show off that power a little bit?

Nope. 23 shutouts and zero pitchers batting practices. Shout out to Brad Bergesen for that one.

-(Laughs) Awesome! At what point is it that you turn to pitching and realize that you're pretty good at it?

I started to notice that I was pretty good about 7th grade or so and then got into high school. Still played a position. Migrated to the outfield, played center field for my entire high school career. But, I think it was as a sophomore in high school when I realized maybe I could really go somewhere, pitching.

-With your loved ones so far away, have you started converting people into Phillies fans?

No, not really. Everybody back home's pretty much a Minnesota Twins fan, 'cause my dad's from Minnesota. So, they're all Twins fans. My cousin, he'll follow the Phillies. He's been a Giants fan his whole life, but ever since I got drafted by the Phillies, he's got a Phillies hat and he's kind of getting into the whole Phillies thing.

-Anybody in your family with other athletic prowess? Anybody else an athlete in the family?

No. I'm an only child, so no siblings. I was the youngest in my family, so everybody's been older than me till recently. I've got a few young cousins. Nobody yet. Maybe the cousins will come along.

-You could groom them and teach them the slugging pitcher ways...show them how to pitch. Show them the new curve!

(Laughs) Yeah. I'll do my best.

Connor Brogdon – Photo – Michael Dill – Michael Dill Photography

Chapter Seven – The Draft and International Signings

The draft was held in early June and the Phillies made 38 selections. They were able to sign 32 of the players chosen. Here's the complete list.

Phillies 2018 Draft Selections

Round 1: (overall pick # 3) - Alec Bohm -JR 3B - Wichita State

Round 2: Pick was forfeited due to signing Carlos Santana

Round 3: Pick was forfeited due to signing of Jake Arrieta

Round 4: (overall pick # 107) - Colton Eastman - JR RHP - Cal State Fullerton

Round 5: (overall pick # 137) - Matt Vierling - JR OF - Notre Dame

Round 6: (overall pick # 167) - Logan Simmons - SS - Tatnall High, Macon, GA

Round 7: (overall pick # 197) - Gabriel Cotto - LHP - Puerto Rico Baseball Academy

Round 8: (overall pick # 227) - Seth Lancaster - JR SS - Coastal Carolina University

Round 9: (overall pick # 257) - Dominic Pipkin - RHP - Pinole Valley HS, Pinole, CA

Round 10: (overall pick # 287) - Madison Stokes - SR 3B - South Carolina University

Round 11: (overall pick # 317) - Jack Perkins -JR RHP - Stetson University

Round 12: (overall pick # 347) - James MacArthur - JR RHP - University of Mississippi

Round 13: (overall pick # 377) - Jose Mercado - SS - Carlos Beltran Baseball Academy HS

Round 14: (overall pick # 407) - Jesse Wilkening - JR C - University of Nebraska

Round 15: (overall pick # 437) - Daniel Carpenter - RHP - Martin Luther King HS - Riverside,CA – Did not sign

Round 16: (overall pick # 467) - Tyler McKay - RHP - Howard Junior College - Texas

Round 17: (overall pick # 497) - Keylan Kilgore - LHP - JR - Wichita State University

Round 18: (overall pick # 527) - Matt Kroon - 3B - JR - Oklahoma State University

Round 19: (overall pick # 557) - Mark Potter - RHP - Central Florida Junior College

Round 20: (overall pick # 587) - Connor Litton - 3B - JR - East Carolina University

Round 21: (overall pick # 617) - Jake Smith - RHP - Chapel Hill High School - North Carolina – Did not sign

Round 22: (overall pick # 647) - Luke Miller - OF - JR - Indiana University

Round 23: (overall pick # 677) - Logan O'Hoppe - C - St John the Baptist HS - New York

Round 24: (overall pick # 707) - Corbin Williams - OF - College of the Canyons Community College

Round 25: (overall pick # 737) - Adam Cox - RHP - SR - Montana State University

Round 26: (overall pick # 767) - Eric White - RHP - SR - Southern Arkansas University

Round 27: (overall pick # 797) - Jack Conley - C - JR - North Carolina State University

Round 28: (overall pick # 827) - Jonathan Jones - RHP - Manville High School – Texas – Did not sign

Round 29: (overall pick # 857) - Jaylen Smith - LHP - Copperas Cove High School - Texas

Round 30: (overall pick # 887) - Branden Ramey - RHP - Martin Luther High School - Riverside, CA

Round 31: (overall pick # 917) - Tyler Carr - RHP - SR - University of South Alabama

Round 32: (overall pick # 947) - Ben Aklinski - OF - SR - University of Kentucky

Round 33: (overall pick # 977) - Jake Kinney - RHP - Tallahassee Community College

Round 34: (overall pick # 1007) - Nick Matera - C - JR - Rutgers University

Round 35: (overall pick # 1037) - Austin Ross - RHP - SR - Radford University

Round 36: (overall pick # 1067) - Trent Bowles - OF -SR - University of Texas-San Antonio

Round 37: (overall pick # 1097) - Ryan Rijo - 1B - New Mexico Junior College – Did not sign

Round 38: (overall pick # 1127) - Stephen Jones - RHP - JR Samford University- Alabama – Did not sign

Round 39: (overall pick # 1157) - Matheu Nelson - C - Calvary Christian High School - Clearwater, FL – Did not sign

Round 40: (overall pick # 1187) - Waylon Richardson – RHP - Kankakee Community College - Illinois

Phillies 2018 Draft Choices by Position and the round they were selected:

First Base: One

Ryan Rijo - 38

Second Base: None

Shortstop: Three

Logan Simmons - 6
Seth Lancaster - 8
Jose Mercado - 13

Third base: Four

Alec Bohm - 1
Madison Stokes - 10
Matt Kroon - 18
Connor Litton - 20

Catcher: Five

Jesse Wilkening - 14
Logan O'Hoppe - 23
Jack Conley - 27
Nick Matera - 34
Matheu Nelson - 39

Outfield: Five

Matt Vierling - 5
Luke Miller - 22
Corbin Williams -24
Ben Aklinski - 32
Trent Bowles -36

LHP: Three

Gabriel Cotto - 7
Keylan Kilgore - 17
Jaylen Smith - 29

RHP: Seventeen

Colton Eastman - 4
Dominic Pipkin - 9
Jack Perkins - 11
James MacArthur - 12
Daniel Carpenter - 15
Tyler McKay - 16
Mark Potter - 19
Jake Smith - 21
Adam Cox - 25
Eric White - 26
Jonathan Jones - 28
Brandon Ramey - 30
Tyler Carr - 31
Jake Kinney - 33
Austin Ross - 35
Stephen Jones - 38
Waylon Richardson - 40

High School Selections: 10
Junior College Selections: 4
College Selections: 24

The International signing period began in July and the Phillies were once again very active. Here's a list of the some of the more notable signings:

Starlyn Castillo, rhp, Dominican Republic (No. 16 prospect)

Fernando Ortega, rhp, Dominican Republic (No. 32 prospect)

Joalbert Angulo, lhp, Venezuela (No. 42 prospect)

Alexeis Azuaje, ss, Venezuela

Andrick Nava, c, Venezuela

Javier Vina, c, Venezuela

Kervin Pichardo, ss, Dominican Republic

Victor Diaz, c, Dominican Republic

Jeury Corona, of, Dominican Republic

Jonathan Rivas, rhp, Venezuela

Reiberth Gil, of, Venezuela

Neyker Ibarra, lhp, Venezuela

Wilson Gherbaz, rhp, Venezuela

Luis Vegas, rhp, Venezuela

Eiberson Castellano, rhp, Venezuela

Curtis Mead, IF, Australia

Bruce Wang, C, China

Rixon Wingrove, 1B, Australia

Hsin-Chieh Lin, rhp, Taiwan

Chi-Ling Hsu, rhp, Taiwan

Yoan Antonac, rhp, France

Mitchell Edwards,C, Australia

Logan Simmons – Photo by Mark Wylie

Mark Potter – Photo by Gail Dull – AKA Baseball Betsy

Alec Bohm – Photo by Mark Wylie

Luke Miller makes the play! – Photo by Mark Wylie

Gabriel Cotto – Photo by Mark Wylie

Logan O'Hoppe – Photo by Mark Wylie

Dominic Pipkin – Photo by Mark Wylie

Jaylen Smith – Photo by Gail Dull – AKA Baseball Betsy

Jake Kinney – Photo by Gail Dull – AKA Baseball Betsy

Trent Bowles

Chapter Eight – Williamsport Crosscutters

The Crosscutters finished the season with a 32-44 record and in a tie for fifth place in the New York Penn League's Pinckney Division. They were 17-21 at home and 26-38 on the road. It was a very young team this year, in fact the youngest position player crew in the league at an average age of 20.1 compared to the league average of 20.9. The pitching staff was also the youngest in the league at an average age of 20.3 compared to the league average of 21.5.

Skipper Pat Borders employed 21 different position players during the summer and 27 different pitchers. He saw four position players get promoted to Lakewood during the year along with four pitchers. Two players were released during the season. Sixteen players joined the club during different parts of the summer after beginning their year in the Gulf Coast League.

The Crosscutter's rankings within the 14-team league:

Offense:

Runs: 12th - 293
Hits: 4th - 603
Doubles: Tied for 6th - 119
Triples: 5th - 23
Home Runs: 8th - 33
RBIs: 10th - 270
Total Bases: 8th - 867
Walks: 12th - 209
Least Strikeouts: 9th - 620
Stolen Bases: 12th - 49
OBP: 12th - .310
Slugging Percentage: 8th - .351
Batting Average: Tied for 6th - .244
OPS: 9th - .661

Pitching:

ERA: 4th - 3.45
Shutouts: 4th - 6
Saves: Tied for 4th - 21
Innings Pitched: 8th - 649.2
Least Hits Allowed: 8th - 585
Least Runs Allowed: 5th - 304
Least Earned Runs Allowed: 4th - 249
Least Home Runs Allowed: 5th - 32
Least Walks Allowed: Tied for 8th - 264
Most Strikeouts: 3rd - 674
WHIP: Tied for 6th - 1.31
Holds: 9th - 15

Individual League Leaders: (in Top 10)

Games: Ben Pelletier - 5th - 69, Jonathan Guzman - Tied for 9th - 62

At Bats: Ben Pelletier - 2nd - 256

Hits: Ben Pelletier - 2nd - 71

Doubles: Ben Pelletier - Tied for 3rd - 17, Danny Mayer - Tied for 9th - 11, Brayan Gonzalez - Tied for 10th - 10

Triples: Ben Pelletier - Tied for 4th - 4, Ben Aklinski & Seth Lancaster - Tied for 5th - 3

Home Runs: Ben Pelletier - Tied for 3rd - 9, Ben Aklinski - Tied for 5th - 7, Danny Mayer - Tied for 9th - 5

RBIs: Ben Pelletier - 2nd - 45

Total Bases: Ben Pelletier - 2nd - 123

Slugging Percentage (min 2.7 PA/League Game): Ben Pelletier - .480 - 3rd, Ben Aklinski - .426 - 9th

Batting Average: (min 2.7 PA/League Game): Rafael Marchan - .4th - .301

OPS: (min 2.7 PA/League Game): Ben Pelletier - 6th - .814

Pitching:

Wins: Randy Alcantara & Francisco Morales - Tied for 4th -4

ERA (min 0.8 IP/League Game): Ethan Lindow - 3rd - 2.19, Manuel Silva - 4th - 2.60

Appearances: Randy Alcantara - 6th - 20, Jose Jimenez - 8th - 17

Saves: Keylan Kilgore - Tied for 1st - 10, Randy Alcantara - Tied for 6th - 4

Innings Pitched: Ethan Lindow - 7th - 70

Strikeouts: Francisco Morales - 3rd - 68, Ethan Lindow - Tied for 7th - 63, Manuel Silva - Tied for 10th - 60

WHIP (min 0.8 IP/League Game): Ethan Lindow - Tied for 4th - 1.10

Holds: Randy Alcantara - Tied for 3rd - 4, Jose Jimenez - Tied for 4th - 3

Standout performers this season:

Ben Pelletier became the first Crosscutters player ever to lead the team in Hits, Doubles, Triples, Home Runs and RBI in a single season. That's quite a feat considering the long history of the franchise and the many major leaguers that played for Williamsport before getting to the show. The 20-year-old, Canadian outfielder posted a .277/.333/.480 slash line with an OPS of .814.

Ben Aklinski (22-years-old) had a solid first pro season posting a .256/.335/.410 slash line in 53 games (204 at bats) with 7 homers and 25 RBIs.

Nineteen-year-old catcher Rafael Marchan impressed all summer both defensively and offensively. He hit .301/.343/.362 in 51 games (196 at bats) with 9 stolen Bases. Marchan also threw out 20 would be base stealers (29 percent).

Matt Vierling (21) and Madison Stokes (22) dominated the NYPL during their brief stays. Vierling hit .420 in 12 games (50 AB's) and Stokes hit .338 in 22 games (77 AB's) before both were promoted to Lakewood where they continued to excel. Both college players were drafted in the top 10 club selections of this year's draft.

Jake Holmes tore up the Gulf Coast League and earned a promotion to Williamsport on August 3rd. The 20-year-old third baseman more than held his own with the Crosscutters and posted a slash line of .252/.330/.272 in 29 games (103 at bats). He's also shown marked improvement at third which is a position he's learned to play exclusively in his brief two-year career.

Alec Bohm, this year's first round pick can flat out hit. That's easy to see when you watch him take BP or in game action. The 22-year-old suffered a knee injury with the Crosscutters on July 14th and didn't return to Williamsport till August 20th after going to Clearwater for a rehab assignment. His numbers were modest in his first pro season but the talent is evident. I saw him more in Fall Instructs and believe that he could skip Lakewood and begin next season with Clearwater.

Edwin Rodriquez is one of my favorite young men in the Organization. He had an all-star season for Williamsport this summer and also spent seven games with Lakewood. The 21-year-old first baseman/outfielder posted a .250/.286/.417 slash line in 34 games (120 at bats) with 3 homers and 25 RBIs for the Crosscutters.

Pitching:

Francisco Morales (18 years old) has all the tools to be a special pitcher. The young man has size (6'4", 185), velocity (94-96 FB), repertoire (FB, Slider, Change) and moxy all on his side. It's a matter of consistency and command that will determine how fast and how far he goes up the ladder. Morales finished the season strong posting a 3.48 ERA in his four post all-star game starts.

Ethan Lindow (20 years old) is a confident and driven young man. He's also got the talent to back up the demeanor. Ethan posted a stellar 2.19 ERA in 13 starts (70 IP) with a 3-2 record this summer. The lefty has good size at 6'3", 180 and a mix of pitches that all play as potential plus pitches.

Manuel Silva has electric stuff, the ability to jump his FB mid 90's, the lefty natural cut on his pitches, and a hook that can play as a plus pitch. The 19-year-old is slender at 6'2", 145 but has great torque in his delivery and the ball pops out of his hand. He posted an excellent 2.60 ERA in 62 1/3 IP this summer and was excellent post all-star break in his four starts with a 1.89 ERA in 19 IP with 19 K's. This kid can pitch.

Randy Alcantara started the year at Lakewood before shifting to Williamsport. He was a New York Penn League all-star. Randy went 4-1 with a 2.15 ERA in 20 games (46 IP) with 29 K's as a multi inning reliever. He's recorded a 2.19 ERA in 90.33 IP over the past two seasons as a Crosscutter.

Jhordany Mezquita is yet another young lefty with a powerful arm. He's capable of sitting mid 90's with his fastball. The 20-year-old will be 21 in January. Once to watch.

James McArthur was stellar as a Crosscutter. The 21-year-old right hander out of Ole Miss pitched in 8 games and recorded a "Little League number" as his ERA. He posted a 0.64 ERA in 28 1/3 IP with 31 strikeouts and didn't allow a run in his last six Crosscutter appearances (23 1/3 IP). He was promoted to Lakewood on August 28th and extended the shutout streak another six innings.

20-year-old lefty Jose Jimenez shifted to the bullpen this year as a multi-inning reliever. He's got good stuff and is fearless. Jose recorded a 3.71 ERA in 17 games (26.2 IP) with 33 K's and 9 walks. He was outstanding in the month of August with a perfect 0.00 ERA in six games (10 1/3 IP) with 12 K's. The young man has an outstanding personality that shines thru, he's in the process of learning English but his smile every time I see him is the universal language.

Keylan Killgore waited a bit to sign after being drafted in the 17th round of this year's draft out of Wichita State. He signed on June 29th and we had the opportunity to chat at Clearwater before he moved up to Williamsport. Keylan was a reliever in college so assuming the closer role for the Crosscutters was a natural fit. He was excellent as he earned 10 saves in 10 chances appearing in 14 games with 29 strikeouts in 22 1/3 IP. He posted a 0.81 ERA and was assigned to Lakewood for the playoffs on September 3rd.

Colton Eastman had his innings limited this year after signing as he pitched 117 2/3 innings during his college season. He did piggy back starts with Williamsport and appeared in 8 games with 18 IP. Colton recorded 23 strikeouts and a 3.00 ERA.

Jack Perkins also saw innings limitations this summer, his first as a pro, as he also had a heavy innings burden during his college season at Stetson where he went 11-3 in 106 IP. Perkins often piggy backed Eastman in the games he appeared in with Williamsport. The 21-year-old righty appeared in 8 games and recorded a 4.50 ERA in 18 games (18 IP) with 18 K's.

Juan Escorcia had a solid season with the Crosscutters. The 22-year-old right hander was an XST surprise, for me at least, as I hadn't seen him pitch previously. He spent his first three pro seasons as a member of the Yankees organization and did not pitch in affiliated baseball in 2017. The Phillies signed him in January of this year. Escorcia has really good stuff. He got pitching coach Hector Berrios excited about his ability. That's not an accomplishment to take lightly. Juan recorded a 3.29 ERA this summer in 41 innings with 49 K's but was even better than that in August when he put up a 2.53 ERA in 21 1/3 IP with 27 K's.

Rafael Carvajal had an excellent summer with the Crosscutters. He was named to the All-Star squad as he recorded a 1.59 ERA in 16 games (34 IP) with 32 K's. Rafael is 22 years old.

A young team this summer for Williamsport that, although they struggled winning games, had a lot of projectable talent. Lakewood should field another strong crew in 2019 as this group moves up the chain.

Seth Lancaster – Photo by Tammi Reibsome

Manny Silva

Ben Pelletier – Photo by Tammi Reibsome

Rafael Marchan – Photo by Tammi Reibsome

Keylan Killgore – Photo by Tammi Reibsome

James McArthur – Photo by Tammi Reisbome

Ethan Lindow – Photo by Tammi Reibsome

Jhordany Mezquita

Madison Stokes – Photo by Tammi Reibsome

Randy Alcantara – Photo by Tammi Reibsome

Jose Jimenez

Chapter Nine – Gulf Coast League – Jim Peyton

Gulf Coast Phillies

The Gulf Coast League is a rookie level league in central and southern Florida. It is comprised of 18 teams in 4 divisions and represents 15 organizations. In 2018 the Phillies became the third organization to sponsor a second team in the GCL. Their GCL Phillies with manager Roly de Armas became the GCL Phillies East. Nelson Prada took over management of the new GCL Phillies West.

This was my seventh summer watching future, hopeful contributors to the Philadelphia Phillies begin their stateside odyssey through one of America's last bastions of indentured servitude, Major League Baseball's minor league system.

I spend a lot of time watching Phillies' prospects as they pass through Clearwater. One of the things I have learned, and it is something that I hope others will consider, is that the Gulf Coast League is a rookie league where the indoctrination of young men into their chosen profession of baseball and the development of their talents are more important that the results on a score board or in a box score.

Each June, high school and college players whom the Phillies signed after their selection during the annual amateur draft, report to the Phillies' Paul Owens Training Facility at the Carpenter Complex in Clearwater. They begin their careers physically more advanced than their Latin American counterparts, but slightly behind developmentally. Most of the Latin players have spent a season on the roster of one of the Phillies' summer teams in the Dominican Summer League. A very few, who weren't on one of the Dominican teams, would have spent months at the Phillies' Dominican Academy that shares facilities with the DSL teams.

When the Phillies' Gulf Coast League team gathers at the Complex, it brings together this diverse group of individuals. The Phillies as an organization in recent years have resisted the urge to make major changes in a new player's approach. Their philosophy had been to allow the newest players, the drafted players, to continue doing things in the ways they had grown comfortable, and wait until the fall instructional league to break down and rebuild their baseball mechanics. Recent changes in player development personnel and the addition and expansion of the analytic and video departments would seem to allow a quicker dissemination of information to players, coaches, trainers, and anyone involved in the development of prospects.

Gulf Coast Phillies East

The GCL Phillies East posted a 30-24 record and finished first in the Northeast division under manager Roly de Armas. A 19-9 stretch through a 5-week period in mid-season provided the Phillies with the lead they would ride to the division title. They were eliminated in a semifinal loss. In addition to de Armas, the staff included hitting coach Rafael DeLima, pitching coach Hector Mercado, and coach Charlie Hayes.

There were 34 players on the team's active roster but including promoted players and rehab assignments as many as 58 players saw action. They were a formidable offensive team. They had the third best batting average (.274), second best slugging percentage (.405), third best on base percentage (.754), and second most HR (37) in the GCL. They had the third youngest pitching staff, the second fewest walks allowed (149), and the best K/BB (2.85).

Many stood out. Two were second baseman Nicolas Torres and catcher Juan Aparicio who were named to the GCL Post Season All-Star team.

Starting Pitchers

Victor Santos is an 18-year-old, right-handed pitcher the Phillies signed as an international free agent out of the Dominican Republic in November, 2016. The 2018 season was his second as a professional, his first stateside. During his 2017 season in the Dominican Summer League, Santos posted a 4-2 record in 12 appearances (9 starts) and a 2.57 ERA. He struck out 38 and walked 5 in 49.0 innings. In his American debut, Santos posted a 6-1 record in 11 starts and a 3.03 ERA. He continued to show good command, striking out 65 and walking 4 in 59.1 innings. He pitched six innings on five occasions. He issued three of his four walks in his third appearance of the season and didn't walk another batter until his 11th start to end the regular season. His best outing was a six-inning, two-hitter in which he struck out eleven and walked none on July 28th. He sported a low 90s fastball and a developing slider and change up.

Dominic Pipkin was the Phillies ninth round pick in the 2018 amateur draft out of Pinole Valley High School (CA). He made his debut on June 27th and pitched 2.0 scoreless innings, allowing no hits, walking one, and striking out three. His best outing was a five inning, one-hitter on July 21st where he walked none and struck out five. Pipken is a 6'4, right-handed pitcher who made 10 appearances, 8 of which were starts. He posted a 1-2 record and 3.64 ERA. He struck out 18 and walked 8 in 29.2 innings.

Jonas De La Cruz is a 20-year-old, right-handed pitcher signed by the Phillies as an international free agent out of the Dominican Republic in September, 2016. He recorded a 5-6 record and 3.71 ERA during the 2017 Dominican Summer League season. He struck out 60 and walked 33 in 63.0 innings, 15 appearances/14 starts. He made 10 appearances/6 starts during his stateside debut with the 2018 Phillies. He posted a 5-2 record and 4.46 ERA. He struck out 31 and walked 19 in 34.1 innings. He'll need to improve on his 5.0 BB/9.

Carlos Francisco is a 20-year-old, right-handed pitcher the Phillies signed as an international free agent out of the Dominican Republic in April, 2017. He was immediately assigned to the Dominican Summer League. Francisco suffered a 1-5 record but posted a 2.70 ERA. He struck out 41 and walked 20 in 50.0 innings. Stateside for the 2018 Phillies, he posted a 2-4 record and 6.51 ERA. He walked 18 in 37.1 innings but struck out 41 for a 9.9 BB/9. He has a low 90s fastball.

Gabriel Cotto is an 18-year-old, left-handed pitcher the Phillies selected in the seventh round of the 2018 Amateur Draft out of the Puerto Rico Baseball Academy. The slightly built Cottto(he's 6'5, 175) shows promise. The Phillies brought him along slowly, two and three inning appearances after a disastrous first start where he hit three batters in one-third of an inning. He showed poise and progressed well enough until another rough outing near the end of the season. He'll need to work on his command. Although he struck out 15 batters in 15.1 innings, he also walked 16 batters and hit six with pitches.

Relief Pitchers

Bailey Cummings is a 20-year-old, right-handed pitcher the Phillies selected in the 29th round of the 2017 Amateur Draft out of San Jacinto North Junior College (TX). He was limited to 2.2 innings in August of his draft year, but excelled as a high leverage reliever in 2018. He went 2-2 with a 1.88 ERA and collected 2 saves. In 24.0 innings, he walked 6 (2.3 BB/9) and struck out 31 (11.6 K/9). He has a sub-90s fastball and a curve ball.

Gabriel Yanez is a 19-year-old, left-handed pitcher the Phillies signed as an international free agent out of Venezuela on January 12, 2017. He threw just 4.0 innings for his DSL team in 2017, but was still brought stateside to pitch in the GCL in 2018. He had a 6.43 ERA in 35.0 innings, but struck out 33 (8.5 K/9) and walked 3 (0.8 K/9. He made 3 starts and 12 relief appearances. He didn't record a win or a loss, but managed 2 saves in 2 save opportunities.

Alejandro Made is a 20-year-old, right-handed pitcher the Phillies signed as an international free agent out of the Dominican Republic on July 2, 2017. After just 6.0 innings for his 2017 DSL team, he was brought to Florida to pitch for the Phillies in the 2018 GCL season. He posted a 4-2 record and 2.66 ERA in 14 relief appearances. He struck out 25 in 23.2 innings (9.5 K/9) and walked 9 (3.4 BB/9). He has a low to mid 90s fastball.

Brian Auerbach is a 22-year-old, right-handed pitcher the Phillies signed as a non-drafted free agent out of Rollins College on June 18, 2018. The Dunedin, Florida native posted a 2-0 record and 1.59 ERA in 13 relief appearances. In 22.2 innings, he struck out 19 (7.5 K/9) and walked just 4 (1.6 BB/9).

Mark Potter is a 20-year-old, right-handed pitcher the Phillies selected in the 19th round of the 2018 Amateur Draft out of Jacksonville University (FL). He posted a 1-0 record and 1.96 ERA in 11 relief appearances. He struck out 4 in 23.0 innings (1.6 BB/9) and struck out 13 (5.1 K/9) while posting a 0.957WHIP.

Eric White is a 22-year-old, right-handed pitcher selected by the Phillies in the 26th round of the 2018 Amateur Draft out of Dallas Baptist University (TX). He posted a 1-0 record and 0.82 ERA in six appearances. In 11.0 innings, he walked one (0.8 BB/9) and struck out 7 (5.7 K/9) while posting a 0.818 WHIP. He has a low 90s fastball.

Taylor Lehman is a 22-year-old, left handed pitcher the Phillies signed as a non-drafted free agent out of Penn State University on June 18, 2018. He posted a 0-1 record with a 7.02 ERA. In 16.2 innings, he struck out 17 batters.

Jake Kinney is a 21-year-old, right-handed pitcher the Phillies selected in the 33rd round of the 2018 Amateur Draft out of Tallahassee Community College. He had made a commitment to attend Florida State but the Phillies were able to lure him away with an offer he couldn't refuse. He signed late and only made seven appearances. The big reliever (he's 6'7, 220) posted a 3.00 ERA in 9.0 innings and struck out eleven. He held opponents scoreless in his first six appearances. He had a low to mid 90s fastball.

Justin Miller is a 20-year-old, right-handed pitcher the Phillies selected in the 12th round of the 2016 Amateur Draft out of Central Union High School (CA). He spent his first two seasons as a reliever, but the Phillies appeared to be stretching him out as a starter in spring training. He posted a 1-5 record with a 4.50 ERA. He struck out 27 in 28.0 innings. He was the victim of some shoddy defense as he was dinged with 13 unearned runs, the first unearned runs of his career. He had an upper 80s to low 90s fastball and a curve ball.

Middle Infielders

Nicolas Torres played this season as an 18-year-old, right-handed hitting second baseman signed by the Phillies as an international free agent out of Venezuela on July 2, 2016. He made his debut in the DSL in 2017 and posted a .333 average with 17 extra base hits. He made his stateside debut this season and started 32 games. He posted a .302/.340/.396/.736 slash with a HR and 19 RBI. In 151 plate appearances, he walked 8 times (5.3%) and struck out 27 times (17.9%). He committed just 3 errors and posted a .977 fielding percentage in 132 total chances. He was recognized for his accomplishments when he was named to the GCL Post Season All-Star team.

Edgar Made is an 18year-old, switch hitting second baseman signed by the Phillies as an international free agent out of the Dominican Republic on July 8, 2016. He made his debut in the DSL in 2017 and posted a .333 average with 17 extra base hits. He made his stateside debut this season and started 32 games. He posted a .302/.340/.396/.736 slash with a HR and 19 RBI. In 151 plate appearances, he walked 8 times (5.3%) and struck out 27 times (17.9%). He committed just 3 errors and posted a .977 fielding percentage in 132 total chances.

Logan Simmons is an 18-year-old, right-handed hitting shortstop the Phillies selected in the sixth round of the 2018 Amateur Draft out of Tattnall Square Academy (GA). He posted a .232/.345/.400/.745 slash but finished the season strong over his last 12 games, batting .353/.436/.706/1.142 (12 for 34) with 3 HR.

Corner Infielders

Jack Zoellner is a 23-year-old first baseman the Phillies selected in the ninth round of the 2017 Amateur Draft out of the University of New Mexico. He was placed on the disabled list after being assigned to the Lakewood BlueClaws. He got a few at bats with the GCL Phillies at the end of the 2017 season. He returned to the GCL in 2018 and spent the entire season there. After posting a .240/.364/.422/.786 slash with seven HR, he was traded to Baltimore for cash considerations in the international free agent market.

Jake Holmes is a 20-year-old, right-handed hitting third baseman the Phillies selected in the eleventh round of the 2017 Amateur Draft out of Pinnacle High School (AZ). Holmes followed a nice 2017 season with an even better 2018 season. He slashed .353/.395/.534/.930 in 31 games before he was promoted to Low-A Williamsport. In 129 plate appearances, he had 4 HR, 29 RBI, 10 walks (7.8%), and 19 strike outs (14.7%). Holmes began his transition from shortstop to third baseman after his 2017 season.

Luke Miller is a 22-year-old, right-handed hitting third baseman the Phillies selected in the 22nd round of the 2018 Amateur Draft out of Indiana University. He posted a .284/.381/.385/.766 slash with 2 HR and 21 RBI. In 126 plate appearances, he walked 17 times (13.5%) and struck out 18 times (14.3%). He is a versatile who also saw playing time at second base, first base, and all three outfield positions.

Outfielders

Julio Francisco is a 20-year-old, left-handed hitting outfielder the Phillies signed as an international free agent out of the Dominican Republic on September 9, 2016. He hit .318 for his DSL team in 2017 and earned a trip stateside for the 2018 GCL season. He slashed .293/.352/.395/.747 in 44 games with 14 steals in 18 attempts. He played 333.2 error-free innings in center field.

James Smith is a 23-year-old, right-handed hitting outfielder the Phillies signed as a non-drafted free agent out of Central Washington University on June 1, 2018. He was the Great Northwest Athletic Conference Player of the Year. He started slow, not getting his first professional hit until his seventh start, but rode a .346 average over the next 35 games to a final slash of .280/.351/.439/.791 with 3 HR and 22 RBI. He drew 13 walks (8.7%) and struck out 23 times (15.4%) in 149 plate appearances. He played all three outfield positions and committed one error in 322.2 innings.

Carlos De La Cruz is an 18-year-old, right-handed hitting outfielder (who turned nineteen in October) the Phillies signed as a non-drafted free agent on August 23, 2017. He began his professional career in 2018 and slashed .284/.345/.459/.805 with 6 HR and 21 RBI. He did strike out in about 1/3 of his plate 165 appearances. He started 40 games in right field and missed about two weeks due to an injury that did not result in a trip to the disabled list. He probably has as much raw power as anyone in the Phillies' minor league system.

Jose Rivera is a 19-year-old, right-handed hitting outfielder the Phillies signed as an international free agent out of the Dominican Republic on March 16, 2017. He posted a

.277/.353/.347/.699 slash. He didn't exhibit much power with just 6 extra base hits, no HR, but showed an ability to get on base with a 10.1 BB/9 (12 walks) and 15.9 K/9 (19 strike outs) in 119 plate appearances. He was versatile playing second and third bases during the season as well as left field.

Ben Aklinski is a 22-year-old, right-handed hitting outfielder the Phillies selected in the 32nd round of the 2018 Amateur draft out of Kentucky University. He played just 10 games in the outfield (LF-8, CF-1, RF-1) before being promoted to Williamsport. In 39 plate appearances, he slashed .267/.410/.300/.710 with 8 walks and 3 strike outs. He had just one extra base hit, but did hit seven at Williamsport.

Catchers

Jack Conley is a 21-year-old, right-handed hitter the Phillies signed as their 27th round draft pick in the 2018 Amateur Draft out of North Carolina State University on June 18, 2018. He caught 27 games, 17 as a starter. He posted a .329/447/.461/.907 slash in 94 plate appearances. He had 2 HR, 11 RBI, 14 BB (14.9%), and 17 K (18.1%).

Carlos Oropeza is a 19-year-old, right-handed hitter the Phillies signed as an international free agent out of Venezuela on January 28, 2016. He spent his first two professional seasons playing with the Phillies' Dominican Summer League teams. In 2018, he caught 25 games, 18 as a starter. He posted a .281/.347/.337/.684 slash. He threw out just 4 of 26 base stealers (15%). He also saw some action at first base (5 starts).

Juan Aparicio is an 18-year-old, right-handed hitter the Phillies signed as an international free agent out of Venezuela on July 2, 2016. He played well enough in his first season in the Dominican Summer League that he was brought stateside for the 2018 GCL season. He saw action in 24 games, 13 starts. He posted a .339/.378/.518/.896 slash with 3 HR and 15 RBI. He threw out 5 of 20 base stealers (20%). At season's end, he was recognized for his accomplishments when he was named to the GCL Post Season All-Star team.

Mitchell Edwards is a 19-year-old, switch hitter the Phillies signed as an international free agent out of Australia on June 8, 2018. He saw limited action in 12 games (5 starts) and posted a .250/.308/.417/.724 slash. He showed feel for the position and threw out 67% of base stealers (6 of 9).

League Leaders

- Wins - Second: Victor Santos (6), Third: Jonas De La Cruz (5)
- Innings Pitched - Second: Victor Santos (59.1)
- K - Second: Victor Santos (65)

Team Leaders

- AVG - Nicolas Torres (.302), Julio Francisco (.293), Carlos De La Cruz (.284)
- Runs -Jack Zoellner (31), Julio Francisco (28), James Smith (27)
- HR - Jack Zoellner (7), Carlos De La Cruz (6), Jake Holmes (4)
- RBI - Jake Holmes (29), Jack Zoellner (26), James Smith (22)
- SB - Julio Francisco (14), Nicolas Torres (7), Jake Holmes (4)
- Wins - Victor Santos (6), Jonas De La Cruz (5), Alejandro Made (4)
- Saves - Brian Auerbach (3), Bailey Cummings (2), Gabriel Yanez (2)
- K - Victor Santos (65), Carlos Francisco (41), Gabriel Yanez (33)
- ERA - Victor Santos (3.03)
- WHIP - Victor Santos (1.13)

Gulf Coast Phillies West

In their initial season, the GCL Phillies West posted a 30-24 record and finished second in the Northwest division, seven-and-half games back under manager Nelson Prada. They remained in contact with first place Tigers West as they steadily increased their lead and weren't officially eliminated until the day after beating the Tigers and pulling within five games with five games left in the season. Their highlight may have been their 5-2 record against Phillies East which included a 19-1 drubbing in the last game between the two teams. West flirted with batting over .300 as a team for a good part of the season. In addition to Prada, the staff included hitting coach Chris Heintz and pitching coach Matt Hockenberry.

There are 37 players on the team's active roster but including promoted players and rehab assignments as many as 54 players saw action. They were a formidable offensive team. They had the best batting average (.289), third best on base percentage (.357), second most runs (301), second most hits (503), most stolen bases (94), second fewest strike outs (346), second most sacrifice hits (18), and most sacrifice flies (24). They had the fourth youngest pitching staff, and one of four complete games in the league. Many stood out.

One stand out performer was shortstop Luis Garcia who was named to the GCL Post Season All-Star team.

Starting Pitchers

Victor Vargas is an 18-year-old, right-handed pitcher the Phillies signed as an international free agent out of Colombia on July 2, 2017. He made his professional debut as a seventeen-year old this summer, and as one of the youngest starting pitchers in the league (fourth youngest among pitchers with at least seven starts). In light of this, he had predictable results - a 1-4 record, 6.00 ERA, 8 HR, and 1.622 WHIP. But, in 45.0 innings, he had a 2.2 BB/9 and a 6.8 K/9. He has an upper 80s fastball and throws a curve ball. His best game was a 5.0 inning start on July 27th. He gave up one run on 3 hits and struck out six.

Ben Brown is a 19-year-old, right-handed pitcher the Phillies selected in the 33rd round of the 2018 Amateur Draft out of Ward Melville High School (NY). Big Ben (he's 6'6, 210) pitched the 2018 season as an eighteen-year old, turning nineteen in September. After throwing just 14.0 innings in his draft year, Brown was inserted into the Phillies' starting rotation in 2018. He posted a 4-2 record and 3.12 ERA. In 49.0 innings pitched, he walked 15 (2.8 BB/9) and struck out 62 (11.4 K/9). His season highlight came on July 24th when he struck out 16 batters in a six inning, two-hit performance. His fastball is improving and is in the upper 80s to low 90s.

Kyle Glogoski is a 19-year-old, right-handed pitcher the Phillies signed as an international free agent out of New Zealand on January 8, 2018. He debuted out of the bullpen and struck out six in 3.1 innings in his first two appearances. He was inserted into the starting rotation and made 8 starts. In 39.0 innings, he posted a 4-0 record and 2.31 ERA with 11 walks (2.5 BB/9), 47 strike outs (10.8 K/9), and a 1.05 WHIP. He throws his fastball in the upper 80s to low 90s, and complements it with a change up and curve ball. His best start came on July 27th when he tossed 6.0 shutout innings while allowing 3 hits and striking out seven.

Rafi Gonell is a 21-year-old, right-handed pitcher the Phillies signed as an international free agent on January 19, 2018 out of the Dominican Republic. Even though he is older, this was his first recorded venture into professional baseball. He posted a 5-1 record with a 4.65 ERA. In 40.2 innings, he struck out 41 (9.1 K/9) but walked 20 (4.4 BB/9). He has a low 90s fastball and a curve ball. His best game was a 5.0 inning start on July second when he shut the opposition down on 2 hits and struck out seven.

Relief Pitchers

Leonel Aponte is a 19-year-old, right-handed pitcher signed by the Phillies as an international free agent out of Venezuela on November 19, 2015. He played his first 2 seasons in the DSL and posted a 2.77 ERA in 2016 and a 1.52 ERA with a 7-1 record in 2017 on his way to selection on the Baseball America DSL All Star Team the same year. He came stateside in 2018 and posted a 3-2 record with a 4.40 ERA mostly as a reliever, striking out 30 in 30.2 innings.

Jose Conopoima is an 18-year-old, right-handed pitcher signed by the Phillies as an international free agent out of Venezuela on March 7, 2017. He posted a 2.04 ERA in the DSL during 2017. He debuted in Florida during the 2018 GCL season with a 1-2 record and a 3.53 ERA. He made 5 starts among his 14 appearances, and was more effective as a reliever with a 3.10 ERA and fewer walks per nine innings (0.9 v. 2.3).

Adam Cox is a 22-year-old, right-handed pitcher the Phillies selected in the 25th round of the 2018 Amateur Draft out of Montana State University and signed on June 12, 2018. He saw action with both GCL teams, and posted a combined 0-2 record with a 2.70 ERA, striking out 21 in 20.0 innings. He held opposing left-handed batters to a 1.58 batting average.

Ethan Evanko is a 23-year-old, left-handed pitcher the Phillies signed as a non-drafted free agent out of Grand Canyon University (AZ) on June 19, 2018. He posted a 2-2 record with a 3.38 ERA and striking out 19 batters in 21.1 innings. His bets outing was a victory in 4.0 innings of long relief where he held the opposition to one run on 3 hits while striking out 5 on July 21st

Blake Bennett is a 22-year-old, right-handed pitcher the Phillies signed as a non-drafted free agent out of Memphis University on June 19, 2018. He posted a 3-1 record with a 1.83 ERA. In 19.2 innings, he struck out 17 batters and walked just 4 (1.8 BB/9). He held opposing left-handed batters to a .211 batting average.

Jaylen Smith is a 17-year-old, left-handed pitcher the Phillies selected in the 29th round of the 2018 Amateur Draft out of Copperas Cove High School (TX) and signed on June 12, 2018. He's a slightly built kid (at 5"11, 170) with a fastball in the upper 80s topping out at 90 mph. In an extremely small sample size, he posted a 0-1 record and 7.11 ERA. But, in 9 of his 11 appearances, he posted a 1.54 ERA in 11.2 innings.

Brandon Ramey is a 17-year old, right-handed pitcher the Phillies selected in the 30th round of the 2018 Amateur Draft out of Martin Luther King High School (CA) and signed on June 18, 2018. He's another slightly built kid (at 6'3, 170). He was limited to 9.0 innings during the season and didn't pitch after July 19th. In that extremely small sample size, he posted a 1-0 record with a 6.00 ERA in 4 appearances. He held opposing batters to a 2.06 batting average, 1.222 WHIP, and struck out 7.0 batter per nine innings pitched.

Middle Infielders

Luis Garcia is a 17-year-old, switch hitting shortstop the Phillies signed as an international free agent out of the Dominican Republic on July 2, 2017. He began his professional career in the 2018 GCL and posted a league leading .369 batting average. His full slash was .369/.433/.488/.921 and the other components were also among the league leaders. He also led the league with 62 hits and was fourth in runs scored with 33. In his 187 plate appearances, he walked 15 times (8.0%) and struck out just 21 times (11.2%). He had 22 multi-hit games - one 4-hit and seven 3-hit games. His best game was on August 3rd when he went 4-5 with a double, HR, and 3 RBI. He had four 3-RBI and one 4 RBI games. He was recognized for his accomplishments when he was named to the GCL Post Season All-Star team

Christian Valerio is an 18-year-old, right-handed hitting second baseman the Phillies signed as an international free agent out of the Dominican Republic on July 2, 2016. His first professional season was in the 2017 DSL. During the 2018 season, he posted a .270/.340/.373/.713 slash with 13 walks (9.0 %) and 22 strike outs (15.3%) in 144 plate appearances. He was a clutch hitter who hit .385 with two outs and .361 with runners in scoring position. He hit 8 of his 11 extra base hits with runners in scoring position including his only HR and 17 of his 18 RBI. His best game came on July 3rd when he went 3-4 with 2 runs scored, 2 doubles, 2 RBI, and a stolen base.

Corner Infielders

Austin "Stoney" O'Brien is a 24-year-old, right-handed hitting first baseman the Phillies signed as a non-drafted free agent out of Oklahoma University on January 8, 2018. He posted a .325/.407/.480/.887 slash with 3 HR and 26 RBI. In 145 plate appearances, he drew 15 walks (10.3%) and struck out 33 times (22.8%). He played mostly at first base, but spent some time in left field. He had 10-multi hit games, and came through in clutch situations hitting .472 with runners in scoring position.

Rixon Taylor-Wingrove is an 18-year-old, left-handed hitting first baseman the Phillies signed as an international free agent out of Australia on April 20, 2018. Originally listed as a catcher, he was switched to first base during extended spring training. He posted a .241/.310/.342/.652 slash with one HR and 8 RBI in 87 plate appearances. He's a big fellow (6'5, 230) who the Phillies spotted with the Sydney Blue Sox in the Australian Baseball League. He hit .429 in the 21 times he led off an inning. His big game came on August 17th when he went 3-5 with a walk, HR, and 4 RBI. He will return to the Sydney Blue Sox for the 2018 ABL season.

D.J. Stewart is a nineteen-year-old, right-handed hitting third baseman the Phillies selected in the 39th round of the 2017 Amateur Draft out of Westminster Christian Academy (MO) and signed on July 6, 2017. Due to his late signing, he saw limited action in the 2017 season. He was a pitcher and shortstop in high school, but was immediately switched to third base by the Phillies. In 2018, he posted a .281/.352/.351/.702 slash. He had an AVG over .300 most of the season until a 1-12 in his final 3 games. His best games was a 2 hit, 2 double, 3 RBI game on July 10th.

Alec Bohm is a 22-year-old, right-handed hitting third baseman the Phillies selected in the 1st round of the 2018 Amateur Draft out of Wichita State University and signed on June 18, 2018. In an extremely small sample size, he posted a .391/.481/.522/1.003 slash with 2 extra base hits and 3 RBI in 27 plate appearances. He was quickly promoted to Williamsport where his season was derailed when he was hit on the knee with a pitched ball and missed 5 weeks of development. His best game in the GCL came in his 4th appearance on June 22nd when he went 3-3 with 2 runs scored and 2 RBI. He was promoted the next day. His remaining GCL stats came during his 7-game rehab before returning to the Crosscutters on August 20th.

Outfielders

Yerwin Trejo is a 21-year-old, right-handed hitting outfielder the Phillies signed as an international free agent out of Venezuela on April 21, 2016. He played two seasons in the DSL and earned a trip stateside for the 2018 GCL season. He posted a .301/.389/.342/.731 slash with 20 RBI and 23 stolen bases in 32 attempts (71.9%). He has been remarkably consistent from year-to-year with improvement at each level. He played 35 of his 50 starts in center field, and covered right field in his other 15 starts. He committed one error in 409.2 innings (.992) and had 4 outfield assists. He had 18 multi-hit games. His best game was one of his three,

3-hit games where he scored a run, collected 2 RBI, and stole 2 bases <u>on July 27th.</u>

Trent Bowles is a 23-year-old, right-handed hitting outfielder the Phillies selected in the 36th round of the 2018 Amateur Draft out of the University of Texas at San Antonio and signed on June 12, 2018. He posted a .256/.309/.353/.662 in 151 plate appearances with 11 walks (7.3%), 33 strike outs (21.9%), and was successful on 9 of 12 steal attempts (75%). He played both corner outfield positions with one error (.986) in 310.2 innings. He came out of the gate quickly and batted .338 through June and July. His best game was a 3-hit, 3 RGI performance <u>on July 28th.</u>

Luis Matos is an 18-year-old, switch hitting outfielder the Phillies signed as an international free agent out of Venezuela on October 13, 2016. He posted a .270/.303/288/.591 in 122 plate appearances. He played predominantly in right field but saw time at all three outfield positions. He batted .290 with runners in scoring position. His best game came <u>on July 19th</u> when he went 3-3 with a run scored and an RBI.

Corbin Williams is a 20-year-old, right-handed hitting outfielder the Phillies selected in the 24th round of the 2018 Amateur Draft out of the College of Canyons Junior College (CA) and signed June 12, 2018. He posted a .289/.348/.325/.673 slash in 95 plate appearances. He walked 7 times (7.4%) and struck out 27 times (28.4%). He split time between center and right fields, committing one error in 223.0 innings (.984). He has top of the order potential with 12 stolen bases in 16 attempts (75%). He had a couple of 3-hit games. His season was cut short when he left a game on August 3rd and didn't play the rest of the season.

Catchers

Abrahan Gutierrez is an 18-year-old, right-handed hitting catcher the Phillies signed as a free agent after MLB voided his Atlanta Braves contract for signing violations. He was signed by the Phillies on March 6, 2018 and is out of Venezuela. The big backstop (he's 6'2, 214) thrived in Clearwater. He posted a .315/.362/.407/.769 slash with one HR and 30 RBI. In 178 plate appearances, he walked 10 times (5.6%) and struck out an incredibly low 16 times (8.98%). In 227.2 innings behind the dish, he committed 3 errors (.988), 2 passed balls, and threw out 10 of 48 base stealers (21%). His best game came on August 17th when he went 2-3 with a double, 2 walks, 4 runs score, and 3 RBI.

Logan O'Hoppe is an 18-year-old, right-handed hitting catcher the Phillies selected in the 23rd round of the 2018 Amateur Draft out of St. John the Baptist High School (NY). He arrived in Clearwater with a very good defensive reputation and proceeded to scald the baseball at the plate. He posted a .367/.411/.532/.943 slash with 2 HR and 21 RBI. In 124 plate appearances, he walked 10 times (8.1%) and struck out 28 times (22.6%). In 148 innings behind the plate, he committed 2 errors (.987), 2 passed balls, and threw out 9 of 27 base stealers (33.3%). He has very good lefty/righty splits. He had a 4-4 game on July 14th, but his best game was on July 23rd when he went 3-4 with 2 runs scored, a triple, HR, and 2 RBI.

Nick Matera is a 22-year-old, right-handed hitting catcher the Phillies selected in the 34th round in the 2018 Amateur Draft out of Rutgers University. In 92 plate appearances, he posted a .224/.348/.303/.650 slash. He drew 13 walks (14.1%) and struck out 17 times (18.5%). In 74.0 innings, he committed 2 errors (.970), 2 passed balls, and threw out 2 of 5 base stealers (40%).

League Leaders

- AVG - First: Luis Garcia (.369)
- OBP - Third: Luis Garcia (.472)
- Runs - First: Yerwin Trejo (40), Fourth: Luis Garcia (33)
- Hits - First: Luis Garcia (62), Third: Yerwin Trejo (59)
- SB - First: Yerwin Trejo (23)
- Wins - Third: Rafi Gonell (5)
- Complete Game - First: Ben Brown (1)
- Strike Outs - Third: Ben Brown (62)

Team Leaders

- AVG - Luis Garcia (.369), Abrahan Gutierrez (.315), YerwinTrejo (.301)
- Runs -Yerwin Trejo (40), Luis Garcia (33), Stoney O'Brien (27)
- HR - Stoney O'Brien (3), Logan O'Hoppe (2), six with (1)
- RBI - Luis Garcia (32), Abrahan Gutierrez (30), Stoney O'Brien (26)
- SB - Yerwin Trejo (23), Luis Garcia (12), Corbin Williams (12)
- Wins - Rafi Gonell (5), Ben Brown (4), Kyle Glogoski (4)
- Saves - Blake Bennett (6), seven with (1)
- K - Ben Brown (62), Kyle Glogoski (47), Rafi Gonell (41)
- ERA - Ben Brown (3.12), Jose Conopoima (3.53)

- WHIP - Jose Conopoina (1.15), Ben Brown (1.18), Victor Vargas (1.62)

Yerwin Trejo – Photo by Mark Wylie

Juan Aparicio – Photo by Mark Wylie

Luis Garcia – Photo by Mark Wylie

Christian Valerio – Photo by Mark Wylie

Double play action – Photo taken by Mark Wylie

Logan O'Hoppe – Photo by Mark Wylie

Kyle Glogoski – Photo by Mark Wylie

Hector Mercado, DJ Stewart and Dominic Pipkin – Photo taken by Mark Wylie

Jake Holmes – Photo by Mark Wylie

Julio Francisco – Photo by Mark Wylie

Corbin Williams – Photo by Mark Wylie

DJ Stewart – Photo by Mark Wylie

Ben Brown – Photo by Mark Wylie

Blake Bennett – Photo by Mark Wylie

Carlos De La Cruz – Photo by Mark Wylie

Abrahan Gutierrez – Photo by Mark Wylie

Luis Garcia – Photo by Mark Wylie

Nicolas Torres – Photo by Mark Wylie

Chapter Ten – Dominican Summer League

The Phillies once again had two teams in the Dominican Summer League (DSL). The teams were designated as Phillies Red and Phillies White.

Phillies Red:

Managed by: Waner Santana

Samuel Hiciano – Hitting Coach

Les Straker – Pitching Coach

The team went 31-40 (.437) during the season and finished in 5th place in the DSL South Division.

Johan Rojas (18 years old) and Wilfredo Flores (18 years old) led the team in batting average as each player hit .320. Rojas led the club in OPS with a .797 mark.

Rojas and Flores stole 19 and 18 bases respectively while Juan Carlos Smith (21 years old) led the club with 24.

Freddy Francisco had a solid season behind the dish hitting .287 in 167 at bats.

Manuel Urias led the club in ERA posting a 1.95 ERA in 60 IP.

The following players were invited to Florida Instructs in September which is a key indicator of gaining a promotion for the following season.

Pitchers:

Cristian Hernandez
Jordi Martinez
Efrain Morales
Nicoly Pina
Yeison Sanchez
Manuel Urias

Position Players:

Freddy Francisco – C
Guarner Dipre – SS
Johan Rojas – OF/2B

Phillies White:

Managed by: Orlando Munoz

Alex Concepcion – Pitching Coach
Homy Ovalles – Hitting Coach

Coaches for both Red and White:

Jesus Tiamo – Catching
Feliberto Sanchez – Pitching
Silverio Navas – Infield

Team White went 39-33 (.542) and finished fourth in the DSL San Pedro Division.

Juan Herrera (18 years old) led the club in batting average with a .278 mark in 151 at bats. Arturo De Freitas (17 years old) led the club in OBP (.394), Slugging (.422) and OPS (.816).

Luis Pacheco (19 years old) led the club in wins with five and posted an outstanding ERA of 2.00 in 63 IP.

Juan Miranda (19 years old) led the team in saves with seven and posted a stellar ERA of 0.99 in 45.2 IP with 48 strikeouts.

The following players were invited to Florida Instructs in
September which is a key indicator of gaining a promotion
for the following season.

Pitchers:

Maikel Garrido
Juan Geraldo
Juan Miranda
Luis Pacheco
Alfonso Puello
Dalvin Rosario

Position Players:

Arturo De Freitas – C
Cesar Rodriquez – C
Juan Herrera – 3B
Jose Cedeno – OF

Juan Miranda – Photo by Mark Wylie

Juan Herrera – Photo by Mark Wylie

Jose Cedeno – Photo by Mark Wylie

Chapter Eleven – Florida Instructional League

Each September to conclude the minor league season a camp is held at Carpenter Complex for select players that's known as Florida Instructs. It's usually first year players who are invited to indoctrinate themselves into what they should expect the following year in spring training. There are also players invited who are coming to learn new positions or have had a good bit of time lost due to injuries. Some guys come to Instructs to get back into form for winter ball.

This year Instructs camp started on September 17th and ran till October 12th. There were 13 games scheduled against other teams also conducting their own Instructs camps. Seventy players were listed on the published roster but another dozen or so made appearances over the four weeks for various workouts. The camp games were managed by Wilmer Reyes and the field coordination was done by Chris Truby.

2018 Camp Observations from this Fan's View:

Innings were limited intentionally for pitchers over the three weeks of game action, most saw three to five frames total at most. That being said, some young arms who caught my attention that I hadn't seen throw before were Gabriel Cotto, Jake Kinney, Efrain Morales, Starling Castillo, Nicoly Pina, and Manuel Urias.

College hitters Matt Vierling, Madison Stokes, Alec Bohm, Ben Aklinski, and Luke Miller all had hard knocks at various points in camp, Aklinski hit two home runs in the final game of the Instructs season.

Catcher Mitchell Edwards continually impressed with his receiving skills, arm and bat. In general, there's a very good group of teen age catchers in the system at present.

Outfielder Carlos De La Cruz continued to shine. He's an impressive all-around player.

Shortstop Luis Garcia can flat out play. This kid could become a very special player. Nicolas Torres and Christian Valerio also look to have bigger upside yet to come.

Good to see Kevin Gowdy, Nick Fanti, and Cole Stobbe back in action. Nick and Kevin each threw in games albeit Gowdy was limited to about 30 pitches in his one outing. Looking forward to seeing them both in spring training.

Outfielder Jose Cedeno and third baseman Juan Herrera are teenagers who just look like they could be players. Very athletic build and actions, would expect they are on GCL rosters next summer.

Other notes:

Jake Scheiner was in camp briefly to work on adding the catching position to his repertoire. He didn't appear in any games.

Sixto Sanchez was in camp the full time. He threw in games twice and flashed 100 on the heater both times. Sixto experienced some soreness in his collarbone so it was decided he would skip winter league ball in the Arizona Fall League. He's expected to be ready to go full bore in spring training.

Adonis Medina and Mauricio Llovera spent some time in camp working on secondary pitches. Each threw briefly in a couple games.

Tyler McKay was awarded the "most improved" pitcher award by the development staff for Fall Instructs. Tyler battled an illness most of the summer which limited him to just 7.1 IP. He's got big league zip with the fast ball, capable of mid to upper 90's. Another one to watch for.

Waylon Richardson threw in a game for the first time during Instructs, the right hander from Indiana also has big arm potential. He was chosen in the 40th round of this year's draft but don't let that mislead you, another pitcher who could make noise in 2019.

Ben Aklinski and me chatting after his 2-homer game – Photo by Mark Wylie

Alec Bohm with Charlie Manuel – Photo by Barb Potter

Sixto Sanchez and Friends – Photo taken by Mark Wylie

Alec Bohm hit – Photo taken by Mark Wylie

Luis Garcia – Photo taken by Mark Wylie

One of our favorite coaches – Greg Brodzinski

Kevin Gowdy – Photo by Gail Dull – AKA Baseball Betsy

Fall Instructs BP – Photo by Steve Potter

Gabriel Cotto and Juan Aparicio – Mark Wylie Photo

Nick Fanti – Photo by Mark Wylie

Mitchell Edwards – Photo by Gail Dull – AKA Baseball Betsy

Ben Brown – Photo by Steve Potter

Tyler McKay

Waylon Richardson

Chapter Twelve – Awards and Statistics

2018 Minor League Playoffs:

Short Season:

Arizona League Championship:

Dodgers defeated Cubs1: 2 games to 1

Gulf Coast League Championship:

Tigers West defeated Cardinals: 2 games to 1

Dominican Summer League Championship:

Rays1 defeated Rangers1: 3 games to 2

Pioneer League Championship:

Great Falls (Rockies) defeated Grand Junction (White Sox): 2 games to 0

Appalachian League Championship:

Elizabethtown (Twins) defeated Princeton (Rays): 2 games to 0

Northwest League Championship:

Eugene (Cubs) defeated Spokane (Rangers): 3 games to 0

New York Penn League Championship:

Tri-City (Astros) defeated Hudson Valley (Rays): 2 games to 0

Low A Level:

Midwest League Championship:

Bowling Green (Rays) defeated Peoria (Cardinals): 3 game to 1

South Atlantic League Championship:

Lexington (Royals) defeated Lakewood (Phillies): 3 games to 1

High A Level:

California League Championship:

Rancho Cucamonga (Dodgers) defeated Visalia (D-Backs): 3 games to 0

Carolina League Championship:

Blue Creek (Astros) defeated Potomac (Nationals) in one game finals due to Hurricane Florence

Florida State League Championship:

Fort Myers (Twins) defeated Daytona (Reds) 3 games to 1

Double A Level:

Eastern League Championship:

New Hampshire (Jays) defeated Akron (Pirates): 3 games to 0

Southern League Championship:

Jackson (D-Backs) defeated Biloxi (Brewers): 3 games to 1

Texas League Championship:

Tulsa (Dodgers) defeated San Antonio (Padres): 3 games to 0

Triple A Level:

International League Championship:

Durham (Rays) defeated Scranton Wilkes Barre (Yankees): 3 games to 2

Pacific League Championship:

Memphis (Cardinals) defeated Fresno (Astros): 3 games to 1

Championships by Organization:

Dodgers – 3
Rays – 3
Twins – 2
Astros – 2
Tigers – 1
Rockies – 1
Cubs – 1
Royals – 1
Jays – 1
D-backs -1
Cardinals – 1

Following are the 2018 system leaders for full season teams for various categories:

Pitchers:

		Wins
Cole Irvin	Lehigh Valley	14
David Parkinson	Lakewood/Clearwater	11
Ramon Rosso	Lakewood/Clearwater	11
Adonis Medina	Clearwater	10
Damon Jones	Lakewood	10
Enyel De Los Santos	Lehigh Valley	10
Addison Russ	Lakewood/Clearwater	9
Drew Anderson	Lehigh Valley	9
Harold Arauz	Reading/Lehigh Valley	9
Ranfi Casimiro	CW/Reading/Lehigh	9
Spencer Howard	Lakewood	9
Tom Windle	Lehigh Valley	9

Starters	Min 100 IP	ERA
David Parkinson	Lakewood/Clearwater	1.45
Ramon Rosso	Lakewood/Clearwater	2.04
Will Stewart	Lakewood	2.06
Cole Irvin	Lehigh Valley	2.57
Enyel De Los Santos	Lehigh Valley	2.63
Ranger Suarez	Reading/Lehigh Valley	2.75
Damon Jones	Lakewood	3.41
Mauricio Llovera	Clearwater	3.72
Spencer Howard	Lakewood	3.78
JoJo Romero	Reading	3.80

Relievers	Min 50 IP	ERA
Brandon Leibrandt	Lehigh Valley	1.42
Addison Russ	Lakewood/Clearwater	1.68
Zach Warren	Lakewood	1.91
Andrew Brown	Lakewood/Clearwater	2.11
Jonathan Hennigan	Lakewood/Clearwater	2.39
Connor Brogdon	Lakewood	2.47
Julian Garcia	Lakewood	2.54
Kyle Dohy	CW/Reading/Lakewood	2.54
Jakob Hernandez	Clearwater	2.80
Pedro Beato	Lehigh Valley	3.04

		IP
Cole Irvin	Lehigh Valley	161.1
Tom Eshelman	Lehigh Valley	140.1
Harold Arauz	Reading/Lehigh Valley	140
Connor Seabold	Clearwater/Reading	130.1
Enyel De Los Santos	Lehigh Valley	126.2
David Parkinson	Lakewood/Clearwater	124.1
Ranger Suarez	Reading/Lehigh Valley	124.1
Ramon Rosso	Lakewood/Clearwater	123.1
Mauricio Llovera	Clearwater	121
Will Stewart	Lakewood	113.2

		Appearances
Pedro Beato	Lehigh Valley	63
Addison Russ	Lakewood/Clearwater	54
Edgar Garcia	Reading/Lehigh Valley	52
Tom Windle	Lehigh Valley	50
Kyle Dohy	CW/Reading/Lakewood	49
Tyler Gilbert	Reading/Lehigh Valley	48
Aaron Brown	Clearwater/Reading	46
Seth McGarry	Reading	45
Luke Leftwich	Reading	44
Jeff Singer	CW/Reading/Lehigh	44

		Saves
Pedro Beato	Lehigh Valley	35
Addison Russ	Lakewood/Clearwater	27
Jeff Singer	CW/Reading/Lehigh	15
Zach Warren	Lakewood	15
Kyle Dohy	CW/Reading/Lakewood	10
Edgar Garcia	Reading/Lehigh Valley	8
Tyler Gilbert	Reading/Lehigh Valley	5
Aaron Brown	Clearwater/Reading	5
Jakob Hernandez	Clearwater	5
Connor Brogdon	Lakewood	5

		K's
Spencer Howard	Lakewood	147
David Parkinson	Lakewood/Clearwater	141
Ramon Rosso	Lakewood/Clearwater	139
Mauricio Llovera	Clearwater	137
Connor Seabold	Clearwater/Reading	132
Cole Irvin	Lehigh Valley	131
Harold Arauz	Reading/Lehigh Valley	125
Adonis Medina	Clearwater	123
Damon Jones	Lakewood	123
Kyle Dohy	CW/Reading/Lakewood	111

		Min 50 IP
		K's per 9 IP
Zach Warren	Lakewood	16.0
Kyle Dohy	CW/Reading/Lakewood	15.0
Spencer Howard	Lakewood	11.8
Jakob Hernandez	Clearwater	11.8
Addison Russ	Lakewood/Clearwater	11.1
Julian Garcia	Lakewood	10.8
Luke Leftwich	Reading	10.4
Connor Brogdon	Lakewood	10.3
David Parkinson	Lakewood/Clearwater	10.2
Edgar Garcia	Reading/Lehigh Valley	10.2
Ramon Rosso	Lakewood/Clearwater	10.2
Mauricio Llovera	Clearwater	10.2
Adonis Medina	Clearwater	10.0

		Min 50 IP
		BB per 9 IP
Kyle Young	Lakewood	1.2
Bailey Falter	Clearwater	1.4
Gustavo Armas	Lakewood	1.6
Will Stewart	Lakewood	1.7
Brandon Leibrandt	Lehigh Valley	1.8
Cole Irvin	Lehigh Valley	2.0
Tyler Gilbert	Reading/Lehigh Valley	2.0
Connor Brogdon	Lakewood	2.1
Addison Russ	Lakewood/Clearwater	2.1
Andrew Brown	Lakewood/Clearwater	2.1

		Min 50 IP
		WHIP
Brandon Leibrandt	Lehigh Valley	0.87
Gustavo Armas	Lakewood	0.87
Addison Russ	Lakewood/Clearwater	0.92
Andrew Brown	Lakewood/Clearwater	0.96
Will Stewart	Lakewood	0.98
Tyler Gilbert	Reading/Lehigh Valley	1.00
Ben Lively	Lehigh Valley	1.00
David Parkinson	Lakewood/Clearwater	1.01
Kyle Young	Lakewood	1.01
Cole Irvin	Lehigh Valley	1.05

		Games Finished
Pedro Beato	Lehigh Valley	56
Addison Russ	Lakewood/Clearwater	48
Jeff Singer	CW/Reading/Lehigh	31
Edgar Garcia	Reading/Lehigh Valley	28
Zach Warren	Lakewood	28
Kyle Dohy	CW/Reading/Lakewood	27
Aaron Brown	Clearwater/Reading	25
Luke Leftwich	Reading	22
Tom Windle	Lehigh Valley	17
Seth McGarry	Reading	16

		Holds
Jonathan Hennigan	Lakewood/Clearwater	10
Jakob Hernandez	Clearwater	8
Josh Tols	Clearwater/Reading	8
Tyler Gilbert	Reading/Lehigh Valley	7
Yacksel Rios	Lehigh Valley	7
Austin Davis	Reading/Lehigh Valley	7
Seth McGarry	Reading	6
Trevor Bettencourt	Clearwater/Reading	6
Hector Neris	Lehigh Valley	6
Edgar Garcia	Reading/Lehigh Valley	5
Connor Brogdon	Lakewood	5
Julian Garcia	Lakewood	5
Grant Dyer	Clearwater	5

Hitters:

		At Bats
Joey Meneses	Lehigh Valley	492
Malquin Canelo	Reading	470
Darick Hall	Clearwater/Reading	468
Adam Haseley	Clearwater/Reading	466
Jake Scheiner	Lakewood	453
Dean Anna	Lehigh Valley	446
Jose Pujols	Clearwater/Reading	441
Arquimedes Gamboa	Clearwater	434
Mickey Moniak	Clearwater	433
Damek Tomscha	Reading/Lehigh	427

		Runs
Adam Haseley	Clearwater/Reading	77
Joey Meneses	Lehigh Valley	75
Dean Anna	Lehigh Valley	73
Mitch Walding	Lehigh Valley	70
Darick Hall	Clearwater/Reading	68
Jose Pujols	Clearwater/Reading	67
Zach Green	Reading/Lehigh	66
Jake Scheiner	Lakewood	65
Malquin Canelo	Reading	63
Austin Listi	Clearwater/Reading	63

		Hits
Joey Meneses	Lehigh Valley	153
Adam Haseley	Clearwater/Reading	142
Jake Scheiner	Lakewood	134
Austin Listi	Clearwater/Reading	133
Jose Pujols	Clearwater/Reading	130
Dean Anna	Lehigh Valley	121
Malquin Canelo	Reading	118
Mickey Moniak	Clearwater	117
Damek Tomscha	Reading/Lehigh	116
Darick Hall	Clearwater/Reading	114

		Doubles
Zach Green	Reading/Lehigh	35
Jake Scheiner	Lakewood	30
Mickey Moniak	Clearwater	28
Joey Meneses	Lehigh Valley	27
Nick Maton	Lakewood	26
Austin Listi	Clearwater/Reading	25
Kyle Martin	Clearwater/Reading	25
Darick Hall	Clearwater/Reading	22
Dean Anna	Lehigh Valley	20
Mitch Walding	Lehigh Valley	20
Danny Ortiz	Lehigh Valley	20

		Home Runs
Darick Hall	Clearwater/Reading	26
Joey Meneses	Lehigh Valley	23
Jose Pujols	Clearwater/Reading	22
Dylan Cozens	Lehigh Valley	21
Deivi Grullon	Reading	21
Zach Green	Reading/Lehigh	20
Mitch Walding	Lehigh Valley	19
Austin Listi	Clearwater/Reading	18
Rodolfo Duran	Lakewood	18
Damek Tomscha	Reading/Lehigh	17

		RBI's
Darick Hall	Clearwater/Reading	87
Austin Listi	Clearwater/Reading	84
Joey Meneses	Lehigh Valley	82
Jose Pujols	Clearwater/Reading	76
Zach Green	Reading/Lehigh	75
Mitch Walding	Lehigh Valley	69
Jake Scheiner	Lakewood	67
Damek Tomscha	Reading/Lehigh	62
Danny Ortiz	Lehigh Valley	61
Deivi Grullon	Reading	59

		Total Bases
Joey Meneses	Lehigh Valley	251
Jose Pujols	Clearwater/Reading	222
Darick Hall	Clearwater/Reading	216
Austin Listi	Clearwater/Reading	214
Zach Green	Reading/Lehigh	214
Jake Scheiner	Lakewood	213
Adam Haseley	Clearwater/Reading	202
Damek Tomscha	Reading/Lehigh	185
Mitch Walding	Lehigh Valley	184
Malquin Canelo	Reading	172

		Walks
Mitch Walding	Lehigh Valley	73
Austin Listi	Clearwater/Reading	62
Arquimedes Gamboa	Clearwater	53
Dean Anna	Lehigh Valley	51
Jake Scheiner	Lakewood	49
Cornelius Randolph	Reading	48
Jose Pujols	Clearwater/Reading	47
Dylan Cozens	Lehigh Valley	46
Nick Maton	Lakewood	43
Kyle Martin	Clearwater/Reading	42

		AB's (min 300 AB's)
		OBP
Austin Listi	Clearwater/Reading	0.412
Mitch Walding	Lehigh Valley	0.390
Jake Scheiner	Lakewood	0.372
Dean Anna	Lehigh Valley	0.367
Jose Pujols	Clearwater/Reading	0.365
Adam Haseley	Clearwater/Reading	0.361
Joey Meneses	Lehigh Valley	0.360
Zach Green	Reading/Lehigh	0.356
Kevin Markham	Lakewood/Clearwater	0.339
Damek Tomscha	Reading/Lehigh	0.334

		(min 300 AB's)
		SLG Pct
Zach Green	Reading/Lehigh	0.532
Deivi Grullon	Reading	0.515
Joey Meneses	Lehigh Valley	0.510
Jose Pujols	Clearwater/Reading	0.503
Austin Listi	Clearwater/Reading	0.502
Rodolfo Duran	Lakewood	0.495
Mitch Walding	Lehigh Valley	0.474
Jake Scheiner	Lakewood	0.470
Darick Hall	Clearwater/Reading	0.462
Adam Haseley	Clearwater/Reading	0.433

		(min 300 AB's)
		Avg.
Austin Listi	Clearwater/Reading	0.312
Joey Meneses	Lehigh Valley	0.311
Adam Haseley	Clearwater/Reading	0.305
Jake Scheiner	Lakewood	0.296
Jose Pujols	Clearwater/Reading	0.295
Zach Green	Reading/Lehigh	0.281
Deivi Grullon	Reading	0.273
Damek Tomscha	Reading/Lehigh	0.272
Dean Anna	Lehigh Valley	0.271
Mickey Moniak	Clearwater	0.270

		(min 300 AB's)
		OPS
Austin Listi	Clearwater/Reading	0.915
Zach Green	Reading/Lehigh	0.888
Joey Meneses	Lehigh Valley	0.870
Jose Pujols	Clearwater/Reading	0.868
Mitch Walding	Lehigh Valley	0.864
Jake Scheiner	Lakewood	0.842
Deivi Grullon	Reading	0.825
Rodolfo Duran	Lakewood	0.800
Adam Haseley	Clearwater/Reading	0.795
Darick Hall	Clearwater/Reading	0.784

		Stolen Bases
Malquin Canelo	Reading	24
Simon Muzziotti	Lakewood	18
Kevin Markham	Lakewood/Clearwater	17
Daniel Brito	Lakewood/Clearwater	16
Luke Williams	Clearwater	14
Roman Quinn	CW/Reading/Lehigh	14
Jake Scheiner	Lakewood	10
Raul Rivas	Clearwater	10
Dean Anna	Lehigh Valley	9
Dylan Cozens	Lehigh Valley	9

		Games
Joey Meneses	Lehigh Valley	130
Darick Hall	Clearwater/Reading	128
Malquin Canelo	Reading	128
Austin Listi	Clearwater/Reading	123
Dean Anna	Lehigh Valley	122
Jake Scheiner	Lakewood	122
Jose Pujols	Clearwater/Reading	121
Mitch Walding	Lehigh Valley	119
Damek Tomscha	Reading/Lehigh	119
Daniel Brito	Lakewood/Clearwater	119

		Triples
Malquin Canelo	Reading	6
Jake Scheiner	Lakewood	5
Adam Haseley	Clearwater/Reading	5
Nick Maton	Lakewood	5
Daniel Brito	Lakewood/Clearwater	4
Raul Rivas	Clearwater	4
Dean Anna	Lehigh Valley	4
Arquimedes Gamboa	Clearwater	4
Jose Pujols	Clearwater/Reading	4
Kevin Markham	Lakewood/Clearwater	3
Roman Quinn	CW/Reading/Lehigh	3
Mickey Moniak	Clearwater	3
Jiandido Tromp	Reading/Lehigh	3
Zach Green	Reading/Lehigh	3
Colby Fitch	Lakewood	3

		Strikeouts
Jose Pujols	Clearwater/Reading	162
Mitch Walding	Lehigh Valley	148
Jhailyn Ortiz	Lakewood	148
Zach Green	Reading/Lehigh	129
Dylan Cozens	Lehigh Valley	124
Jan Hernandez	Reading	120
Darick Hall	Clearwater/Reading	118
Arquimedes Gamboa	Clearwater	111
Malquin Canelo	Reading	110
Joey Meneses	Lehigh Valley	110

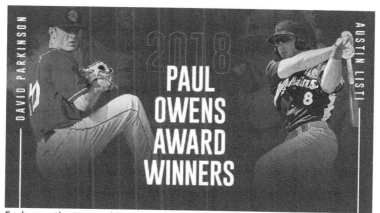

Each year the top position player and pitcher are awarded the Paul Owens Award – the 2018 winners were David Parkinson and Austin Listi

Lehigh Valley Award Winners:

Pedro Beato was named an International League All-Star
Gary Jones was named league Manager of the Year
Cole Irvin was named the league's Outstanding Pitcher
Joey Meneses won the league's MVP Award

David Parkinson and Austin Listi with Gabe Kapler on the day they received Paul Owens Awards in Philadelphia at CBP

Each year the Phillies honor a player from each of the affiliates for community service. The 2018 winners are pictured. This year Lee McDaniel was also awarded the newly named Richie Ashburn & David Montgomery Special Achievement Award, it's the highest employee honor and goes to the employee who best exemplifies the namesakes of the award. Congrats fellas!

Lee McDaniel – Minor League Operations Director
Cole Irvin – Lehigh Valley
Damek Tomscha – Reading
Luke Williams – Clearwater
Danny Mayer – Williamsport
Zach Warren - Lakewood

311

Chapter Thirteen – It's Personal

This chapter is to share with you all some of our personal interactions and to highlight some friends we've made. My wife and I have the good fortune of being retired and able to enjoy baseball every day. We are also fortunate to be able to attend many games and to get to know quite a few of the players, coaches, support staff, front office folks and family members. It's made being a fan more intimate. This chapter is a look at some of the interactions for us this season and a few of the folks we've gotten to know.

We are at Carpenter most every day from January thru mid-October, there's seemingly always someone there working on some facet of the game. Two of the coaches that we've gotten to know a bit are Dickie Noles and Ray Burris. Both were part of 2018 Phillies Phantasy Camp. Dickie is always welcoming. He's one of the most genuine folks we've come to know in the Phillies Organization. He's the employee assistance professional. He is certified as such and is the player's counsel when they have issues. Dickie's a good guy for that as he's always seemingly positive and upbeat. We enjoy chatting with him each time we see him. Ray Burris is the rehab pitching coach and works full time out of the Complex. He also helps out with drills during training camps and is my favorite to watch conducting those. He keeps them light and fun by incorporating nicknames for the players and providing a constant chatter during the drills. We get to chat with him every now and then. He's got a great perspective on baseball and teaching, a true asset to the organization.

Joe Jordan, Player Development Director, parted ways with the Phillies in September. We got to know him over the past four years, Joe would always say hello and chat. He allowed me to present ideas to him via correspondence and then we'd discuss them. A few were actually adopted in some form which was cool. Personally, I'll miss Joe and I wish him well in his next endeavor. I've since met Josh Bonifay who was hired in October to replace Jordan. Josh took the time to chat with us at the Complex, he seems very genuine and sincere, I think he's gonna do very well.

We met Bryan Minniti for the first time in Fall Instructs and he's also very personable and interactive. He's one of my new email buddies! I have a list of front office and baseball operations folks with whom I correspond. Well I write my observations and they amuse me by occasionally reading them. That's a better way of putting it! John Brazer, the Director of Fun and Games, does a pre-game radio show each Sunday on WBCB 1490 and used a weekly minor league standouts list I would diligently send him on Saturday evenings on his broadcasts this year. The big-league announcers also occasionally will use some of the minor league game notes I send them on the television broadcasts. I think it's cool and I appreciate it. It makes me feel a small part of the reporting equation.

We've also become friends with many of the support personnel at the Complex. Security, ushers and store clerks like Mike, Gary, John, Woody, Joe, Bernie, Don, Mark, Dianne, Pat, Josh and Terry are folks who are all welcoming. It's been our privilege to get to know them.

This year we attended the home opener at CBP with my son Nolan and daughter in law Amber. We got to be part of the on field welcoming committee for the team. That was a neat experience.

For the past two summers I've won the online Phillies ALS auction event enabling me to have dinner with team president Andy MacPhail. It's been great both years as my wife and I along with four guests we choose get to come to CBP, have dinner with him in the executive dining room and then enjoy a ballgame. Mr. MacPhail allows me to chat about all things baseball although the focus inevitably turns to the minor leagues, my chosen "expertise". He's very personable and I truly enjoy the couple hours we chat about Phillies baseball. I must make an impression as he remembers me when I see him in spring training!

Two of the players we have gotten to know a bit along with some of their family members are Austin Listi and Darick Hall. This summer my daughter and son-in-law hosted a barbecue at their house and the fellas came. My mother-in-law, Eleanor, had a tough winter as she contracted pneumonia and was later diagnosed with cancer as well. At my request, Austin and Darick went with my wife and I to visit "Mom-Mom" after the barbecue at her retirement center. It was a huge lift for her as she's a big Phillies fan that the two players took time out of their day to see her, really cool.

Later that summer I asked Scott Palmer, Phillies Public Relations Director, if he would be willing to visit Eleanor along with the Phanatic at the retirement center. Without hesitation he said yes and August 20th became a very special day for a lot of folks. Here's what I wrote about that day the morning afterwards.

8/21/18: The Impact of Laughter and Entertainment

Yesterday the Phillie Phanatic and Scott Palmer visited the Simpson Meadows Retirement Community in Downingtown. My Mother-In-Law Eleanor (we call her Mom-Mom) lives there. She's had a tough go of it the past few months and I wanted to do something special for her this summer. My wife and I reside in Clearwater, Florida now but we came up north here to visit with her for the months of July and August.

In July, two terrific young men who play for the Reading Fightin's, Austin Listi and Darrick Hall, came to our family barbecue on one of their off days at my daughter's house. While at the barbecue I asked them if they would go see Mom-Mom with me as well. They never blinked in their agreement to do so. They sat and chatted with her and it really made a very special lady feel great. She's a big fan of the Phillies and told them so. At first, she didn't believe me when I told her they would come but was so delighted when they did. I thought it was really cool that they did that.

Word got around the Community and many of the other residents were disappointed that the ball players weren't able to say hello to them. I told Mom-Mom how about if I try to get the Phillie Phanatic to come visit? She said "no way the Phanatic would come to see her!" Each of my articles I post on my Phillies blog, I also happen to send to a group of various Phillies employees and contacts of various positions in the organization. One of them happens to be the Phanatic's best friend.

I wrote a note to Scott Palmer and Tom Burgoyne and asked how I could arrange for a Phanatic visit. They put me in contact with a very nice young lady named Andrea Guest. Andrea arranged for a date that the Phanatic indeed could come to Simpson Meadows. My next step was to tell Mom-Mom and Simpson Meadows. I met a nice lady named Eileen who is the event coordinator at Simpson Meadows and we arranged for the visit to happen.

It would be August 20th, an off day for the club. I asked Mr. Palmer if he might be able to attend, to my surprise and delight he said he would be happy to do so. Mom-Mom was still in disbelief.

Eileen spread the word throughout the Simpson Meadows community and at 2:30 on a Monday afternoon we were set for the visit. It was tremendous, the Phanatic was spectacular. There were folks lined up in the hallways and also in the main meeting room of the facility. The Phanatic didn't miss a one of them. Smiles and laughter were abundant. It was very cool how folks reacted. Scott did a great job describing and directing, and Eileen was also outstanding leading the big green fella around and snapping pictures. Eleanor was interviewed by Scott and the Phanatic took pictures with her and family members in attendance. It was very emotional for me. It was an hour that brought two things I love together, my family and my baseball club. It was so very, very cool!

Today we went back to visit Mom-Mom and so many people stopped us to thank us for bringing Scott and the Phanatic to Simpson Meadows. We were told by staff, residents and family members alike that it had a tremendous impact on them, that for some it was a dream come true, and that many hadn't laughed so hard in a long while. The Phanatic was brilliant in his performance and the beaming reactions were evident of that. He touched many, many funny bones but also hearts. Can't thank Mike (the dude inside the big green yesterday) enough for what he did for those people.

I already knew Mr. Palmer was a really sincere and good guy. To drive to Chester County and emcee the event was even more evidence of that. From the bottom of this old ballplayer's heart thanks to Scott, Mike and Andrea for the visit. I hope you all know what an impact it had on all the folks' lives that were there. They will be beaming and telling stories about it for years to come! My Mom-Mom was so very happy as well. Those folks do special stuff. It's much, much more than just entertainment. They touched people in the most positive of ways. I can't ever say enough thanks for that!

Happy Day, Happy Baseball indeed!

My wife and I attended multiple games this summer, GCL, Threshers, Fightin's and the Phillies both in Tampa and at CBP. One of the highlights was the retirement of Ryan Howard's jersey in Reading. His wife and children were on hand and the Big Piece was gracious and forthcoming as he's always been. He had a spectacular career which was cut down by injuries, the numbers were still amazing!

A great summer of baseball for us, wanted to share it a bit with you all, in particular the "family" feel we get from our interaction with the organization. It's one of the qualities I hope the team never loses, it's really fun to experience.

Jim Peyton, Dickie Noles and myself chatting baseball – Photo by Mark Wylie

Darick Hall, Mom-Mom Eleanor Graul and Austin Listi

The Phanatic and Scott Palmer with Mom-Mom Eleanor

Me with team President Andy MacPhail

Logan Moore and me during January workouts

Ryan Howard and his daughter at the Reading retirement ceremony

My sons Dan and Nolan and son in law Matt and I have attended Phantasy Camp together twice, pictured here with Milt Thompson, Ryan Howard, Mariano Duncan and Ricky Jordan. What an honor to join family with my Phillies fan passion!

Opening Day – CBP on the red carpet!

My son Nolan and his wife Amber at Opening Day

My wife Barb with one of our favorite ushers Mike Brodsky

Gary Kay is a little league volunteer who makes the trek to Williamsport from Clearwater each year, he's also a great Security team member at the Complex

Frank and Danie Berlingis – Threshers season ticket holders

Hulk Hogan was at Spring Training, here he's with my son in law Matt and grandson Isaac

My daughter Michelle and our friend Vivian Mott enjoying the Threshers
VIP seats at Spectrum Field

Gail and Steve Dull – AKA Baseball Betsy and Ross

My wife Barb with Joe, another favorite usher of ours!

Dave Anderson and Jim Peyton – lifelong Phillies fans

My wife Barb and Don – our favorite usher of all time!

Gotta see these ladies at the Threshers store – Diane and Pat

Cindi – Delco's Original Steaks owner, our favorite vendor – Spring Training – check out their store in Dunedin – you won't be disappointed!

Spring Training Buddies – my daughter Michelle and her mom Barb

One Potter meets another – me chatting with Mark Potter

One of my favorites Will Hibbs, injuries held him back in 2018, looking for a bounce back season in 2019

With Austin Bossart in Reading

Me and young star Luis Garcia

A family dinner with McKenzie Mills and Darick Hall – my daughter's Michelle and Kristen, grandson Isaac, son in law Matt and granddaughter Aislynn

Mark Wylie, Ben Pelletier, Darick Hall, me, Austin Listi, Jim Peyton, Barb Potter and Tracy Peyton after dinner at The Salt Rock Grille during Fall Instructs

Host families are a big part of the minor league process. Following are a few photos of some player hosts I've gotten to know a bit from Williamsport and Lakewood.

Tyler Carr with host parent Sue Nicholas Storm – Williamsport

Gustavo Armas with host family David and Barbara Alexander and their twin sons Sean and Christopher – Lakewood

Ramon Rosso with Michael Dolcemascolo, Michael's mom and grand
parents have been long time host families in Lakewood

Chapter Fourteen – System Outlook

The Phillies Minor League system once again posted a positive winning percentage. The nine teams combined for a record of 474-405 (.539). The organization had four teams (Lehigh, Clearwater, Lakewood and GCL East) qualify for their respective league playoffs. Lakewood went to the championship series in the South Atlantic League. While winning games isn't the sole objective of player development, I believe it's very important to establish a winning way. The club has done that consistently over the past three seasons. They finished 2018 in the top five for winning percentage for overall system, US Affiliates only (.549) and for full season squads (.565). From my perspective that bodes very well.

A few words on some players who either came back from previous injury in 2018 or suffered a setback that now puts them in rehab mode. RHP Jose Taveras is working hard to come back to the form he showed in 2017, last season was a lost summer for him. The big right hander, if healthy, would be another solid arm in the system. My young friend Sutter McLoughlin retired this past season due to shoulder issues, he was a reliever, we wish him well going forward in his off field endeavors.

LHP Anton Kuznetsov required TJ surgery this past summer, he's working his way back with coach Burris. Three guys who look to make impressions in 2019 are RHP Grant Dyer, RHP Kevin Gowdy and infielder Cole Stobbe, Gowdy and Stobbe were back on the field during Instructs as mentioned. Dyer returned to action on June 20th after a long recovery from TJ surgery, he last pitched prior to that on September 3rd, 2016. Grant got into seven games with the Threshers in 2018 and looks to get back to his old form next season. We hope all the players who suffered injury set backs a swift and full recovery and will look to see them soon back in action.

Many analysts and publications have the system as a top tier program amongst the thirty major league clubs. From our view, we concur with that opinion. There's tremendous depth. And while some may feel there is a lack of top tier talent, this observer feels there are players who could develop into that category.

The big club will continue to improve with trades and free agent signings but there's a solid avenue of improvement as well from the minor leaguers who progress to the show. In 2018, seven players who were developed in the Phillies minor leagues made their major league debuts with the Phillies. They followed fourteen who had done so in 2017. There's more talent to come and 2019 should also present its share of big-league debuts.

Analytics are the norm now in baseball, it's expected that in 2019 the usage of analytics will be pushed even more throughout the Phillies Minor League System and new approaches will be explored. I think the staff and players are ready for the challenge of that incorporation and will continue to excel. The outlook is very good from this fan's view as we go into the 2019 season and beyond. I have a saying I use for many of my blog postings. I foresee using it a lot, Happy Day, Happy Baseball!

Talent, analytics, coaching, and performance. It's all part of it. We're on the right track!

Following is a list of every Phillies minor league system player (in alphabetic order) who either was signed to a minor league contract prior to this publication or played extensive time in the Phillies Minor League system during the 2018 season. I have not included players on the major league 40-man roster that played the majority of their time in the big leagues in 2018. The list shows each player's position, their playing age for the majority of the 2019 season, and where I'd project them to play the 2019 season at the time of this writing (November, 2018). There are 325 players listed, apologies if I've omitted anyone. It's the most comprehensive list I could compile.

Happy Day, Happy Baseball!

Name	Position	2019 Projection
Aklinski, Ben	OF	LWD - 22 yrs old
Alastre, Jesus	OF	CW - 22 yrs old
Alcala, Bryan	RHP	GCL/WPT - 21 yrs old
Alcantara, Randy	RHP	LWD - 22 yrs old
Aleman, Edinson	LHP	DSL - 18 yrs old
Alfonso, Victor	2B	DSL - 19 yrs old
Angulo, Joalbert	LHP	DSL - 17 yrs old
Anna, Dean	SS	Free Agent - 33 yrs old
Antequera, Jose	OF	CW - 23 yrs old
Antonac, Yoan	RHP	GCL/WPT - 18 yrs old
Aparicio, Juan	C	WPT/LWD - 19 yrs old
Aponte, Leonel	RHP	GCL/WPT - 19 yrs old
Aponte, Ruben	RHP	DSL - 22 yrs old
Araujo, Alexis	RHP	DSL/GCL - 20 yrs old
Arauz, Harold	RHP	Free Agent - 24 yrs old
Arauz, Osvaldo	RHP	DSL - 19 yrs old
Aris, Abdallah	RHP	WPT/LWD - 22 yrs old
Arjona, Kyle	RHP	GCL/WPT - 22 yrs old
Armas, Gustavo	RHP	LWD/CW -23 yrs old
Ascencio, Ryan	C	DSL - 20 yrs old
Astudillo, Hermes	RHP	DSL - 17 yrs old
Auerbach, Brian	RHP	WPT/LWD - 22 yrs old
Avendano, Eudiver	RHP	GCL - 20 yrs old
Azuaje, Alexeis	SS	DSL - 17 yrs old
Azuaje, Jesus	IF	WPT/LWD - 21 yrs old

Barboza, Edward	C	DSL - 18 yrs old
Barreto, Freddy	C	DSL - 19 yrs old
Beato, Pedro	RHP	Free Agent - 33 yrs old
Bennett, Blake	RHP	LWD - 23 yrs old
Betancourt, Carlos	RHP	DSL/GCL - 18 yrs old
Bettencourt, Trevor	RHP	REA - 24 yrs old
Bido, Nathaniel	LHP	DSL - 22 yrs old
Blanco, Jeison	RHP	DSL - 21 yrs old
Bocio, Keudy	OF	LWD - 20 yrs old
Boekhoudt, Mani	OF	DSL/GCL - 19 yrs old
Bohm, Alec	3B	CW/REA - 22 yrs old
Bossart, Austin	C	LH - 25 yrs old
Bowles, Trent	OF	WPT/LWD - 24 yrs old
Brazon, Jose Emiliano	RHP	DSL - 19 yrs old
Brito, Daniel	2B	CW/REA - 21 yrs old
Brogdon, Connor	RHP	CW/REA - 24 yrs old
Brown, Aaron	LHP	LH - 27 yrs old
Brown, Andrew	RHP	LWD/CW - 21 yrs old
Brown, Benjamin	RHP	WPT/LWD - 19 yrs old
Cabral, Edgar	C	REA - 23 yrs old
Cabrera, Ismael	RHP	CW/REA - 25 yrs old
Candelo, Luis	RHP	DSL/GCL - 21 yrs old
Canelo, Malquin	SS	Free Agent - 24 yrs old
Canizales, Antonio	RHP	DSL - 21 yrs old
Carr, Tyler	RHP	LWD - 23 yrs old
Carrasco, Luis	RHP	CW -24 yrs old

Carvajal, Rafael	RHP	LWD - 22 yrs old
Casimiro, Ranfi	RHP	Free Agent - 26 yrs old
Castellano, Eiberson	RHP	DSL - 17 yrs old
Castillo, Starlyn	RHP	GCL -17 yr old
Cedeno, Jose	OF	GCL - 18 yrs old
Cedeno, Luis	RHP	CW -24 yrs old
Cleavinger, Garrett	LHP	REA - 25 yrs old
Conley, Jack	C	WPT/LWD - 22 yrs old
Conopoima, Jose	RHP	GCL/WPT - 19 yrs old
Corona, Jeury	OF	GCL - 17 yr old
Cotto, Gabriel	LHP	GCL -19 yrs old
Cowgill, Colin	OF	Free Agent - 33 yrs old
Cox, Adam	RHP	WPT/LWD - 23 yrs old
Cozens, Dylan	OF	LH/PHL 25 yrs old
Cruz, Cristofer	RHP	DSL - 20 yrs old
Cumana, Grenny	UTL	REA - 23 yrs old
Cummings, Bailey	RHP	WPT/LWD - 21 yrs old
De Freitas, Arturo	C	GCL - 18 yrs old
De La Cruz, Carlos	OF	WPT - 19 yrs old
De La Cruz, Jonas	RHP	WPT - 21 yrs old
De La Rosa, Maximo	1B	DSL - 20 yrs old
Diaz, Victor (16)	C	DSL - 17 yrs old
Diaz, Wilerik	RHP	DSL/GCL - 22 yrs old
Dipre, Guarner	SS	GCL -18 yr old
Dohy, Kyle	LHP	REA/LH -22 yrs old
Duran, Christopher	3B	DSL - 18 yrs old

Duran, Rodolfo	C	CW - 21 yrs old
Dyer, Grant	RHP	CW/REA - 23 yrs old
Eastman, Colton	RHP	LWD/CW - 22 yrs old
Edwards, Mitchel	C	GCL/WPT -19 yr old
Encarnacion, Jefferson	OF	DSL - 17 yrs old
Escalante, Kevin	C	GCL -19 yrs old
Escorcia, Juan	RHP	LWD - 23 yrs old
Eshelman, Tom	RHP	LH - 24 yrs old
Estevez, Engel	RHP	DSL - 19 yrs old
Evanko, Ethan	RHP	WPT/LWD - 23 yrs old
Fallwell, Tyler	RHP	LWD/CW - 23 yrs old
Falter, Bailey	LHP	REA - 22 yrs old
Fanti, Nick	LHP	CW - 22 yrs old
Fitch, Colby	C	CW/REA - 23 yrs old
Flores, Wilfredo	2B	GCL -19 yrs old
Francisco, Carlos	RHP	DSL - 21 yrs old
Francisco, Freddy	C	GCL - 18 yrs old
Francisco, Julio	OF	WPT/GCL - 21 yrs old
Gamboa, Arquimedes	SS	CW/REA - 21 yrs old
Garcia, Alex	RHP	WPT - 22 yrs old
Garcia, Edgar	RHP	LH/PHL - 23 yrs old
Garcia, Julian	RHP	CW/REA - 24 yrs old
Garcia, Luis	SS	LWD - 18 yrs old
Garcia, Wilbert	OF	DSL - 19 yrs old
Garrido, Maikel	LHP	GCL - 19 yrs old
Geraldo, Juan	RHP	GCL - 17 yr old

Gherbaz, Wilson	RHP	DSL - 17 yrs old
Gil, Reiberth	OF	DSL - 17 yrs old
Gilbert, Tyler	LHP	LH/PHL 25 yrs old
Glogoski, Kyle	RHP	WPT/LWD - 20 yrs old
Goins, Ryan	UTL	Free Agent - 31 yrs old
Gomez Michael	RHP	WPT - 22 yrs old
Gomez, Jose	IF	CW/REA - 22 yrs old
Gomez, Luis	RHP	DSL - 18 yrs old
Gonell, Rafi	RHP	WPT - 22 yrs old
Gonzalez, Brayan	2B	WPT - 19 yrs old
Gonzalez, Oscar	1B	DSL - 18 yrs old
Gonzalez, Reiwal	RHP	DSL/GCL - 24 yrs old
Gowdy, Kevin	RHP	GCL/WPT - 21 yrs old
Green, Zach	1B/3B	Free Agent - 25 yrs old
Grullon, Deivi	C	LH - 23 yrs old
Guthrie, Dalton	IF	CW/REA - 23 yrs old
Gutierrez, Abrahan	C	WPT/LWD - 19 yrs old
Guzman, Jonathan	SS	WPT - 19 yrs old
Guzman, Michael	LHP	DSL - 18 yrs old
Hall, Darick	1B	REA/LH -23 yrs old
Hallead, Tyler	RHP	LWD - 24 yrs old
Hammer, J.D.	RHP	CW/REA - 24 yrs old
Haseley, Adam	OF	REA/LH -23 yrs old
Hennigan, Jonathan	LHP	REA - 24 yrs old
Henriquez, Jesus	IF/OF	WPT/LWD - 21 yrs old
Hernandez, Carlos	C	DSL - 18 yrs old

Hernandez, Christian	RHP	GCL - 17 yrs old
Hernandez, Jakob	LHP	REA - 23 yrs old
Hernandez, Jan	OF	LH - 24 yrs old
Hernandez, Jevi	3B	DSL - 20 yrs old
Hernandez, Joan	RHP	DSL - 19 yrs old
Herrera, Alexis	RHP	DSL/GCL - 20 yrs old
Herrera, Juan	3B	GCL - 19 yrs old
Herrera, Lizardo	RHP	GCL -19 yrs old
Hibbs, Will	RHP	CW/REA - 24 yrs old
Holmes, Jake	3B	LWD - 20 yrs old
Howard, Spencer	RHP	CW/REA - 22 yrs old
Hsu, Chi-Ling	RHP	GCL - 18 yrs old
Ibarra, Neyker	LHP	DSL - 17 yrs old
Irvin, Cole	LHP	LH/PHL 25 yrs old
Jerez. Albert	SS	DSL - 18 yrs old
Jimenez, Jose	LHP	LWD - 21 yrs old
Joel Valdez	LHP	DSL - 17 yrs old
Jones, Damon	LHP	CW/REA - 24 yrs old
Killgore, Keylan	LHP	LWD/CW - 22 yrs old
Kinney, Jake	RHP	WPT/LWD - 22 yrs old
Kroon, Matt	IF	LWD/CW - 22 yrs old
Kuznetsov, Anton	LHP	Injured - 21 yrs old
Lancaster, Seth	IF	LWD/CW - 22 yrs old
Lartigue, Henri	C	REA - 24 yrs old
Leftwich, Luke	RHP	LH - 24 yrs old
Lehman, Taylor	LHP	WPT/LWD - 23 yrs old

Leibrandt, Brandon	LHP	Rehab - Injured - 26 yrs old
Liendo, Wilberson	RHP	DSL/GCL - 19 yrs old
Lima, Christian	RHP	DSL - 18 yrs old
Lin, Hsin-Chieh	RHP	GCL -20 yrs old
Lindow, Ethan	LHP	LWD - 21 yrs old
Lino, Gabriel	C	Free agent - 26 yrs old
Liriano, Elias	RHP	DSL - 20 yrs old
Listi, Austin	OF	LH/PHL 25 yrs old
Litton, Connor	3B	WPT/LWD - 22 yrs old
Llovera, Maricio	RHP	REA - 23 yrs old
Made, Alejandro	RHP	WPT - 21 yrs old
Made, Edgar	2B	GCL -19 yrs old
Maldanado,Omar	RHP	WPT/LWD - 23 yrs old
Marcano, Rafael	LHP	DSL/GCL - 19 yrs old
Marcelino, Oscar	RHP	WPT/LWD - 21 yrs old
Marchan, Rafael	C	LWD - 20 yrs old
Markham, Kevin	OF	REA - 25 yrs old
Marrero, Emmanuel	IF	REA - 26 yrs old
Martin, Kyle	1B	REA - 26 yrs old
Martinez, Alejandro	RHP	DSL - 21 yrs old
Martinez, Jordi	LHP	GCL - 18 yrs old
Martinez, Nerluis	C	WPT - 23 yrs old
Martinez, Robinson	RHP	LWD/CW - 21 yrs old
Mata, Cesar	OF	DSL - 19 yrs old
Mateo, Gregorix	RHP	DSL - 22 yrs old
Matera, Nick	C	WPT - 22 yrs old

Maton, Nick	SS	CW/REA - 22 yrs old
Matos, Luis	OF	GCL/WPT - 19 yrs old
Matos, Malvin	OF	WPT/LWD - 22 yrs old
Mayer, Danny	OF	LWD - 23 yrs old
McArthur, James	RHP	LWD - 22 yrs old
McBride, Matt	1B/C	Free Agent - 34 yrs old
McGarry, Seth	RHP	LH/PHL 25 yrs old
McKay, Tyler	RHP	LH/PHL 25 yrs old
Mead, Curtis	IF	GCL -18 yr old
Medina, Adonis	RHP	REA - 22 yrs old
Mejia, Hernando	RHP	DSL - 19 yrs old
Mendez, Juan	C	GCL/WPT - 20 yrs old
Mendoza, Carlos	OF	DSL - 18 yrs old
Meneses, Heiker	IF	Free agent - 27 yrs old
Meneses, Joey	1B/OF	Free Agent - 27 yrs old
Mercado, Jose	SS	GCL -19 yrs old
Mercedes, Yefferson	LHP	DSL - 20 yrs old
Mezquita, Jhordany	LHP	LWD - 21 yrs old
Middlebrooks, Will	IF	Free Agent - 30 yrs old
Miller, Justin	RHP	WPT/LWD - 21 yrs old
Miller, Luke	IF	LWD - 22 yrs old
Mims, Brian	UTL	CW/REA - 23 yrs old
Miranda. Juan	LHP	GCL/WPT - 20 yrs old
Moniak, Mickey	OF	REA - 21 yrs old
Moore, Logan	C	Free Agent - 28 yrs old
Mora, Raymond	OF	DSL - 18 yrs old

Morales, Efrain	RHP	GCL - 18 yrs old
Morales, Francisco	RHP	LWD - 19 yrs old
Moreno, Noelis	RHP	DSL/GCL - 20 yrs old
Mujica, Luiggi	2B	DSL - 19 yrs old
Muzziotti, Simon	OF	CW - 20 yrs old
Naranjo, Yosmel	LHP	DSL - 19 yrs old
Nava, Andrick	C	DSL - 17 yrs old
Nieporte, Quincy	1B	CW - 24 yrs old
O'Brien, Austin	1B	LWD - 25 yrs old
O'Hoppe, Logan	C	WPT/LWD - 19 yrs old
Omana, Enmanuel	SS	DSL - 21 yrs old
Oropeza, Carlos	C	GCL/WPT - 20 yrs old
Ortega, Fernando	RHP	DSL - 18 yrs old
Ortega, Junior	OF	DSL - 19 yrs old
Ortiz, Danny	OF	Free Agent - 29 yrs old
Ortiz, Jhailyn	OF	LWD/CW - 20 yrs old
Pacheco, Luis	RHP	GCL - 20 yrs old
Palacio, Jose	LHP	DSL - 19 yrs old
Parkinson, David	LHP	REA - 23 yrs old
Parraga, Roger	RHP	DSL - 18 yrs old
Peguero, Giuseppe	OF	DSL - 18 yrs old
Pelletier, Ben	OF	LWD - 20 yrs old
Perez, Daivin	LHP	DSL - 20 yrs old
Perez, Jose	RHP	DSL - 21 yrs old
Perkins, Jack	RHP	LWD - 21 yrs old
Pichardo, Kervin	SS	DSL - 17 yrs old

Pina, Nicoly	RHP	GCL -19 yrs old
Pineda, Leandro	OF	DSL - 17 yrs old
Pipken, Dominic	RHP	WPT/LWD - 19 yrs old
Potter, Mark	RHP	WPT/LWD - 21 yrs old
Prada, Santy	RHP	DSL - 19 yrs old
Puello, Alfonso	RHP	GCL - 18 yrs old
Pujols, Jose	OF	REA/LH - 23 yrs old
Quinn, Blake	RHP	REA - 25 yrs old
Ramey, Brandon	RHP	GCL - 18 yrs old
Ramirez, Luis	RHP	LWD - 21 yrs old
Randolph, Cornelius	OF	REA/LH -22 yrs old
Requena, Alejandro	RHP	CW/REA - 22 yrs old
Reyes, Andy	RHP	DSL - 19 yrs old
Richardson, Waylon	RHP	GCL/WPT - 22 yrs old
Rickles, Nick	C	Free Agent - 29 yrs old
Rivas Aldemar	RHP	DSL - 20 yrs old
Rivas, Jonathan	RHP	DSL - 17 yrs old
Rivas, Raul	IF	REA - 22 yrs old
Rivera, Jose	OF	WPT/GCL - 20 yrs old
Rivero, Alexis	RHP	REA/LH - 24 yrs old
Rivero, Gregori	C	CW - 23 yrs old
Rodriguez, Cesar	C	GCL - 18 yrs old
Rodriguez, Edwin	1B/OF	LWD - 21 yrs old
Rodriguez, Lenin	C	WPT - 21 yrs old
Rojas, Johan	OF	GCL - 18 yrs old
Rojas, Luis	IF	GCL/WPT - 19 yrs old

Romero, JoJo	LHP	REA/LH -22 yrs old
Rondon, Carlos	SS	DSL - 17 yrs old
Rondon, Ellian	SS	DSL - 18 yrs old
Rosario, Dalvin	RHP	GCL - 18 yrs old
Rosario, Sandro	RHP	DSL - 23 yrs old
Ross, Austin	RHP	WPT/LWD - 24 yrs old
Rosso, Ramon	RHP	CW/REA - 23 yrs old
Russ, Addison	RHP	REA - 23 yrs old
Sanchez, Mario	RHP	REA/LH - 24 yrs old
Sanchez, Sergio	LHP	DSL - 18 yrs old
Sanchez, Sixto	RHP	REA - 20 yrs old
Sanchez, Yeison	RHP	GCL/WPT - 21 yrs old
Santa Cruz, Sati	RHP	WPT - 22 yrs old
Santos, Juan	RHP	DSL - 22 yrs old
Santos, Victor	RHP	GCL/WPT - 18 yrs old
Scheiner, Jake	IF/OF	CW/REA - 23 yrs old
Seabold, Connor	RHP	REA - 23 yrs old
Segovia, Eduar	RHP	DSL/GCL - 18 yrs old
Silva, Manuel	LHP	LWD - 20 yrs old
Silva, Wilman	C	DSL - 22 yrs old
Simmons, Logan	SS	GCL/WPT - 19 yrs old
Singer, Jeff	LHP	LH - 25 yrs old
Smith, James	OF	WPT - 23 yrs old
Smith, Jaylen	LHP	GCL - 19 yrs old
Smith, Juan Carlos	1B	DSL - 21 yrs old
Sobil, Victor	RHP	GCL/WPT - 22 yrs old

Stankiewicz, Drew	IF	REA/LH -22 yrs old
Stephen, Josh	OF	REA - 25 yrs old
Stewart, D.J.	3B	WPT - 20 yrs old
Stewart, Will	LHP	CW - 21 yrs old
Stobbe, Cole	3B	LWD - 21 yrs old
Stokes, Madison	IF	CW - 23 yrs old
Suarez, Ranger	LHP	LH/PHL - 23 yrs old
Sutera, Tom	RHP	GCL/WPT - 22 yrs old
Taveras, Jose	RHP	LH - 25 yrs old
Taylor-Wingrove, Rixon	1B	GCL/WPT - 20 yr old
Tejada, Junior	LHP	WPT/GCL - 22 yrs old
Tirado, Alberto	RHP	Free Agent - 24 yrs old
Tols, Josh	LHP	REA/LH - 29 yrs old
Tomscha, Damek	IF/OF	LH - 27 yrs old
Torres, Alberto	LHP	DSL - 18 yrs old
Torres, Nicolas	2B	WPT/LWD - 18 yrs old
Tortolero, Jose	SS	DSL/GCL - 19 yrs old
Trejo, Yerwin	OF	WPT - 22 yrs old
Tromp, Jiandido	OF	Free Agent - 25 yrs old
Urias, Manuel	RHP	GCL - 18 yrs old
Valdez, Jean Carlos	RHP	DSL - 21 yrs old
Valdez, Wilson	3B	DSL - 19 yrs old
Valentin, Jesse	IF	Free Agent - 25 yrs old
Valerio, Christian	2B	GCL/WPT - 19 yrs old
Vargas, Victor	RHP	GCL/WPT - 18 yrs old
Vegas, Luis	RHP	DSL - 17 yrs old

Ventura, Ezequiel	RHP	DSL - 16 yrs old
Vierling, Matt	OF	CW - 21 yrs old
Vilchez, Daniel	RHP	DSL - 18 yrs old
Vina, Javier	C	DSL - 16 yrs old
Viza, Tyler	RHP	LH/PHL 24 yrs old
Walding, Mitch	3B	LH/PHL 26 yrs old
Wang, Bruce	C	GCL -19 yrs old
Warren, Zach	LHP	CW/REA - 22 yrs old
White, Eric	RHP	WPT/LWD - 23 yrs old
Wilkening, Jesse	C	LWD/CW -22 yrs old
Williams, Corbin	OF	GCL/WPT - 21 yrs old
Williams, Luke	IF/OF	REA - 22 yrs old
Windle, Tom	LHP	LH - 27 yrs old
Yanez, Gabriel	LHP	GCL - 19 yrs old
Young, Kyle	LHP	LWD - 21 yrs old
Key : WPT - Williamsport		
GCL : Gulf Coast League		
DSL : Dominican Summer League		
LWD : Lakewood		
CW : Clearwater		
REA : Reading		
LH : Lehigh Valley		
PHL : Phillies 40 man roster		